Bernardo Olivera, OCSO

The Sun at Midnight

*Monastic Experience
of the
Christian Mystery*

MONASTIC WISDOM SERIES: NUMBER TWENTY-NINE

The Sun at Midnight

Monastic Experience
of the
Christian Mystery

By

Bernardo Olivera, OCSO

Translated by
Augustine Roberts, OCSO

α

Cistercian Publications
www.cistercianpublications.org

LITURGICAL PRESS
Collegeville, Minnesota
www.litpress.org

A Cistercian Publications title published by Liturgical Press

Cistercian Publications
Editorial Offices
Abbey of Gethsemani
3642 Monks Road
Trappist, Kentucky 40051
www.cistercianpublications.org

1   2   3   4   5   6   7   8   9

Library of Congress Cataloging-in-Publication Data

Olivera, Bernardo.
    The sun at midnight : monastic experience of the Christian mystery / By Bernardo Olivera ; translated by Augustine Roberts.
        p. cm. — (Monastic wisdom series ; 29)
    Includes bibliographical references.
    ISBN 978-0-87907-029-8 — ISBN 978-0-87907-477-7 (e-book)
        1. Mysticism. 2. Cistercians—Spiritual life. 3. Monastic and religious life. I. Roberts, Augustine, 1932– II. Title.

BV5082.3.O45 2012
255'.12—dc23

                                                                2012015410

Contents

Foreword

This new book by Dom Bernardo Olivera owes its paradoxical title, *The Sun at Midnight*, to the nature of mystical language. The title brings to mind the spectacular sight of the winter sky in the Far North, but "midnight" points, above all, to our human experience of searching amid shadows and darkness. "Sun" obviously refers to our longing for light. In the present case, it is a question of the supreme Sun, "the dawn from on high,"[1] the *Kyrios*, the Risen Lord. Thanks to him, our human darkness and death have been mortally wounded by Life. In other words, the present book is based on *Christian experience*. Even more concretely, it concerns *monastic experience*.

Don't be afraid of this, however, in case you are not a monk or a practicing Christian. The author is convinced that there is a mystical presence in you, that you yourself are a mystic who perhaps is unaware of it. Mysticism is deeply human, a foundational experience not belonging exclusively to this or that religion, because it antedates them. Bernardo states this very clearly, insisting that it is more like human love itself, which is everyone's heritage and is lived by many persons in the married state when they experience it as something transcendental, beyond the territory defined by confessions and creeds. So the subject of mysticism touches us all.

Paragraph 41 of Paul VI's *Evangelii Nuntiandi* contains a reflection first addressed to the members of the Council on the Laity on October 2, 1974: "Modern man listens more willingly to witnesses than to teachers, and if he does listen to teachers, it is

---

[1] Lk 1:78.

because they are witnesses." It is in this sense that I want to assure you that Bernardo is a good teacher whose depth of conviction points to his being a fervent witness. What he lives is the silent proclamation of what he is teaching.

Bernardo Olivera, born in Buenos Aires, Argentina, in 1943, was elected abbot general of the Reformed Cistercians, or Trappists (OCSO), on September 8, 1990. From that day until his resignation eighteen years later, we witnessed the almost excessive intensity of his service to the communities of our Order. One of the underlying themes of this service has been spiritual renewal according to the culture of a specific place and time. This, in turn, obliged the Order to look at the challenges that the world of today makes to our identity as believers and monks. When I say "the world of today," I am thinking not of the difficulties that can come from "outside" but rather of those springing from inside ourselves, as children of our age.

Challenges of the World Today

These challenges that the world makes to our identity as Christians, and as monks and nuns, are in a particular way *individualism, hyperactivity,* and *superficiality.* Individualism eats into the quality of community life; hyperactivity undermines contemplative life; and superficiality weakens any commitment to serving the Lord.

Individualism means "closing oneself in, believing oneself to be the center." Only Christ is the center of the community. It is he who calls us together, who makes it possible to have a "common" will, decentralizing us and thus despoiling us of our own will. The individualistic person is the one who is convinced that he or she is the necessary, irreplaceable center, as can happen even in the life of a superior.

Hyperactivity is "much ado about nothing." One has to act, of course. Any commitment—and the contemplative life is one—demands that we give ourselves wholeheartedly to the task at hand. However, any other activity that does not help or flow from such commitments can be suspected of concealing a void that the person is desperate to fill. We know how "busy" everyone is. No one has time enough, everyone is in a hurry; but how do they "fill" their time?

Superficiality involves not "sinking roots." Today's ease of movement and communication results in not having time to let our experiences ripen and our wine become mellow. That is why there is no time for deep roots to grow and become serious, stable commitments. But with deeper roots, it then becomes possible to face the storms, be up to date, stride into the future, and rejoice in one's own culture.

For Benedict of Nursia, the monastery is meant to be a human space, a little world, a context for lived experience. Values and convictions are communicated by a joyful, transparent osmosis, as any psychologist or sociologist can verify. However, to give oneself wholeheartedly to the Master in this "school of the Lord's service" and to have the children really experience the love of their Father, there has to be a "family home" where the brothers live as sons and nothing is preferred to Christ in this "school of Christ." This homey environment is community, which the Benedictine and Cistercian tradition has always looked on as a school of love transforming the monk or nun into the image of Christ.

Experience of the Risen One

His intense activity in promoting this reality in the complex world of our time has made Dom Bernardo live in a state of continual motion. By his countless trips, he has been personally present to the communities, accompanying then by listening wisely and carefully according to the general guidelines he has seen they should follow. He has become a living witness to the human search for God in the monastic way of life.

But what is the strong point of this very special witness for our communities? Soon after being elected abbot general, he replied by saying, "I think I can answer as follows: my strong point is being able to witness to the constant, active presence of the Risen One and of his Mother in the bosom of the Church, and to have a keen sense of humor."

Pastoral realism, a positive byproduct of a thousand and one problems, has turned him—whether he likes it or not—into a living fire extinguisher and, above all, has made him share in the Paschal Mystery those problems embody. This intense pastoral experience takes us back to September 8, 1990, when he first presented himself and his plans as abbot general to us. Perhaps even more, it takes us back to September 8, 1962, the day he entered as a member of the community of Our Lady of the Angels, the Cistercian monastery near Azul, Argentina. That entrance was, in turn, the result of a key vocational experience that had taken place the previous June 28, on the basis of which he understood that he should dedicate his entire life to *listening to the heartbeat of God*, in dead earnest and with a keen sense of humor. These are, indeed, signs of a good witness!

"Jesus, the Christ, is in the deepest recess of my heart. He dwells in me by faith and by the mysterious presence of one risen from the dead. He is always present and acting. His word is true and I can bear witness to it: 'I am with you always, to the end of the age.'" This was one of the "seven words" by which Bernardo showed us what lay in his heart when he sent his first circular letter to the entire Order. So it is not surprising that the collection of his many interventions in different places during the first part of his service as abbot general bears the title *Discipleship, Communion, Mystery*.

Yes—first and foremost, mystery! Out of it necessarily flows Christian mysticism: "It is no longer I who live, but it is Christ who lives in me" (Gal 2:20). From the wealth of teachings, insights, and examples offered to us by Bernardo on these subjects throughout the present book, I would like to emphasize those contained in his chapters on "Our Life's Purpose," "Initial Clarifications," and the longer one on "Our Mystical Experience." These pages contain a splendid, easily accessible summary of mystical theology in the Cistercian school, analyzing it first in its rich human, biblical, and doctrinal connotations, then according to its seven most typical expressions as these are lived among Cistercian mystics, with reference also to other Christian men and women of God. Besides quoting the most representative texts on each type of experience from the monks of the twelfth century and the less known nuns and "holy women" of the thirteenth century, the author's own comments and analyses of their inner meaning are noteworthy.

Underlying the emphasis in these and all chapters on personal mystical experience, we discover the following thesis: *personal mystical experience is not only the key to an adequate renewal of monastic life today, but also—and above all—the foundation, the originating point, of any and all religion or religious tradition.* Mystical experience is, in particular and above all, the origin of Christianity and its rich mystical tradition, which explains the importance of another important chapter of the book, on "Christ, the Supreme Mystic." As the author says, "There is nothing more Christian than Christ's own experience of the Mystery!"

Bernardo's conviction on this point explains the central place occupied by his chapter on mystical experience in the Cistercian school, which otherwise might appear to be excessively lengthy. In fact, the whole work could bear the title *Christian Mystical Experience: A Key to the Future.* It is doubtless because of its importance that Bernardo has wanted the book to be separate from everything else he has written as abbot general. And, due to its particular importance for formation, it is going to be followed by a similar one, more specifically dealing with the experience of the *sponsalia*, that is, the spousal relationship with God in the Risen Christ, the divine Bridegroom.

I would like to conclude by using another phrase from Bernardo that sums up, in my opinion, the fruit of experiencing the Mystery—namely, that it "satisfies the deepest desires of the human heart." It also expresses the joyful reason that led him to write the book in the first place—that is, that mysticism is *good for humanity.* We should all be mystics. The divine point of departure is God's initiative, his overflowing grace. Everyone baptized is a mystic, every person is a mystic, every monk is a mystic. The divine Sun wants to become the living experience of our dark, anxious Midnight, of our search in the "dark night."

I wonder how and when we come to notice the presence of the Mystery. When does it actually *humanize us by making us divine* from the inside? It could be when we live—fully and humanly—situations that are *impossible* for humans but not for God. For example, there are highly dangerous situations that challenge human existence, such as despair, mortal grief, responsibilities with unknown and uncontrollable consequences, broken lives, or questions about the future. And nevertheless, these can be, and are, lived as somehow fulfilling and humanizing, if they are accepted in a not-so-easy peace, serenity, joy, trust, and even consolation: They are then lived freely as a gift, as something welcomed and freely embraced. The strength that one receives to accept them in this way is not subject to any explanation or control. It is a Presence.

In one of his writings, Karl Rahner begins a list of such situations, which he himself invites the reader to extend:

- When there is *complete hope* that is stronger than any particular hope and extends itself in gentle silence as a promise governing all growth and all failures

- When *a responsibility* is freely accepted and carried out without having a clear perspective of success or usefulness

- When a person recognizes and accepts his or her *ultimate freedom* that no earthly power can take away

- When one calmly accepts *falling into the darkness of grief and death* as the beginning of a promise that surpasses our understanding

- When one accepts as good *the total sum of all one's life* that one cannot evaluate on one's own, but which Another has accepted as good despite one's lack of evidence to prove it

- When *a broken experience of love, beauty or joy* is lived simply and accepted as a promise of higher Love, Beauty and Joy, without falling into skeptical cynicism as a cheap buffer against final desolation

- When *daily life* in its bitter, frustrating cruelty is lived serenely and faithfully to the end, accepted in a strength whose origin we cannot see or control

- When you take *the risk of praying while surrounded by silent darkness*, knowing that you are always heard, even when there is no evident reply

- When you *give yourself unconditionally* and your self-surrender is a lived victory

- When *you fall* and your fall means that you can stand up taller than ever

- When you experience *despair* and you mysteriously feel consoled without a consoling reason

- When you entrust your *knowledge and your questions to the silent, saving Mystery*, loved above our shreds of knowledge that have become useless and too small

- When we *try to die every day* and attempt to live as we would like to die: calmly and peacefully

In the context of today's thirst for mystery, these situations speak convincingly about God. Their language is understood. As Javier Vitoria says in *Iglesia Viva*, man will find God today not primarily in the tensions of his needs and lacks, but rather in the fullness of his being and living.

Having arrived here with you, dear reader, it is time to leave you in the good company of a book. I have no doubt about the fruit you will receive from slowly reading the present work. The Spirit of the Risen Lord is waiting in your heart that you may experience a brilliant SUN AT MIDNIGHT.

Santiago Fidel Ordóñez, OCSO
Sobrado—Rome
Easter Sunday
April 12, 2009

Chapter 1

Cultural Context

Cultures

From its very beginning, the Cistercian charism was able to give an acculturated response to the needs of the Church and the world of its time, but the success of the whole Cistercian venture can only be explained by what was in its very roots, namely, *mystical experience*. Today's deepest needs are not so different from those of the twelfth century, which explains why our medieval mystics are so relevant to our culture in its thirst for mystery and new experiences. However, it is not enough that *they* were mystics: we ourselves should be mystics, too. And we will be, if we open our hearts to the work of the Spirit and collaborate with him, since

> this [mystical] way of thinking about God does not lie at the disposal of the thinker. It is a gift of grace, bestowed by the Holy Spirit who breathes where he chooses, when he chooses, how he chooses and upon whom he chooses. Man's part is continually to prepare his heart by ridding his will of foreign attachments, his reason or intellect of anxieties, his memory of idle or absorbing, sometimes even of necessary business.[1]

So it would be good to look at an overview of today's highly mobile culture and at the place in it that is occupied by the religious phenomenon. Then it will be easier to understand the importance

---

[1] William of Saint-Thierry, *The Golden Epistle* 251. (Please see the selected bibliography on pages 130–36 for full references to primary and secondary sources.)

of mysticism for humankind's future and the challenge this confronts us with.

We must first clarify what the word "culture" means. There is no doubt in my mind that culture should not be thought of as something

- *aristocratic*, as if it were just for a few persons "of culture," relegating most of us to the category of "uncultured";

- *European*, feeling that all non-Westerners are uncouth;

- *acquired*, as if the possession of material goods, knowledge, or know-how guaranteed it.

Culture, on the contrary, is intrinsic to the human being. Only humans "cultivate" their three-dimensional relationships: with God (by religion and worship), with their brothers and sisters (in languages, sociability, politics, and the like), and with creation (through economics, work, technology, or art). That is why the word "culture," in its anthropological sense, means a particular way in which a group of people or persons in general cultivate their relationship with nature, among themselves, and with God, thus being able to achieve a fully human level of true life.

Each group of people has its own culture, which is why we can speak of cultures in the plural. Each one of us is, at one and the same time, offspring and parent of the culture in which we live. Thanks to our own culture, we live humanly, but because of it we are limited in what we live. Each person exists in a concrete culture, but our culture does not explain all we are or do, since there is something in us that transcends culture.

It is also possible to speak of "subcultures" in reference to groups that are differentiated by reason of gender (masculine or feminine cultures), vocation (monastic culture or military culture), or places (urban or rural culture). There is, too, an intrinsic link between religion and culture, a link that has been confirmed by different branches of science and scientists, by anthropology (Geertz), sociology (Eliade), and hermeneutics (Ricoeur). So it is not surprising that UNESCO, in its 1982 *Declaration on Cultural Policies*, unanimously recognized that the concept of culture includes spiritual "value systems, traditions and beliefs."

But we can go one step further. The essential part of any culture, its root, is the attitude with which a group of people affirms or denies its religious link with God, that is, its religious values. The fact is that religion bears directly on the ultimate meaning of human existence, offering answers to the most basic existential questions. In this sense, religion gives inspiration to all the other dimensions of culture by opening them to what is transcendent. But if this is so for religion in general, it is even truer for mysticism, since mysticism is the experience that gives birth to religion.

The themes and realities of present-day culture are debatable, especially at a time of transition like the present one. Yet their study cannot be avoided, above all because it tries to diagnose the real situation. In this connection it helps to approach the structural reality of any culture from a triple perspective:

- its infrastructure—the economic element

- its superstructure—the political element

- its omnistructure—the cultural element

And we can add one more item to what we have already said. In the last twenty years the world is experiencing a steady weakening of its politics but a gradual increase of interest in its culture, and this greater emphasis on cultural elements is principally a return to what is religious. So, just as in recent centuries the crisis of religion favored politics, now the reverse is happening: a general political crisis is favoring religion, and consequently mysticism.

Before continuing, it will be necessary to say something here about the phenomenon of modernity and postmodernity.

Modernity

"Modernity," in a broad sense, refers to the last five centuries of Western history. It can be divided into three successive historical periods. The sixteenth and seventeenth centuries were preparatory ones, laying the ground for the eighteenth century, the "Enlightenment," followed by the rapid development that took place during the nineteenth and twentieth centuries. Modernity in the strict sense would extend from the French Revolution until the student upheavals of May 1968 or the energy crisis of 1973. The causes of modernity would include

- the geographical discoveries that placed Europe in a global context; *imperialism*

- the Reformation, which strengthened the sense of each individual's personal conscience as opposed to the simple principle of authority;

- the Copernican-Galilean revolution that took us out of the center and placed us in the cosmos;

- the development of the experimental sciences leading to contemporary technology;

- reflexive philosophy, which questioned the accepted vision of man's relationship to persons and things;

- capitalism as a rational method for producing material goods.

To sum up, the two chief characteristics of modernity are its stress on the autonomy of the person, in opposition to any form of subjection, and its emphasis on the use of reason, as opposed to any form of religiosity or faith. Modern thought can—though risking an oversimplification—be condensed into five key words:

- *reason,* which was given divine status during the French Revolution

- *humanity,* which is more than the sum total of all peoples, states or nations

- *history*—that is, time lived as a unity of continual progress

- *emancipation* from all ignorance, dogmas, authorities, lack of empowerment, and so forth

- *progress,* in the optimistic sense of unending growth that lets utopias blossom

At present, especially in the North Atlantic countries of the West, modernity is lived as a daily reality in four basic ways: in the fragmentation of culture, in the plurality of differing points of view, in experiencing the economy as the center of social life, and in the passage from personalization to individualism. Not everyone lives or has lived the process of modernity as something personal, but shares instead—or has shared—in it insofar as it has been exported from the North Atlantic. Nevertheless, there are still a few groups of people rooted in different forms of pre-modernity, and a few others that "modernize" their culture without necessarily integrating the spirit and values of modern culture.

Postmodernity

It is not easy to speak about postmodernity for the simple reason that postmodernity does not exist. It is in the state of becoming. Rather than being an object to be examined, it is a frame of mind, a way of acting, a vibrant tone that started with the young people of the North Atlantic and is gradually expanding throughout the world.

Some thinkers tell us that postmodernity is a modernity that has been defeated but not replaced. Defeated modernity means that it is neither productive nor creative of anything new, since its major strengths are worn out. Postmodernity is unreplaced modernity because it still feeds on modernity, though without its strongly attractive myths. In such a case, it would be a one-sided reaction to the many one-sided features of modernity, or a sincere desire for a new order in view of modernity's collapse.

In their search for more light on the subject, others distinguish at least three types of postmodernity. Thus they can speak about neoconservative postmodernity, resistance, and disillusionment:

- *Neoconservative postmodernity* is, above all, a defensive reaction on the part of a consumer-oriented system of production that sees itself endangered. It is a reaction within Western capitalist countries as they face their own crisis, with the accent placed on the economic factor, whose health must be improved by increasing each company's assets and production and privatizing nationalized industries. On the level of the ordinary man in the street, this type of postmodernity is expressed in slogans such as "You get what you fight for: push!" "He who does not compete never grows," "Work that is not effective, competitive, and profitable is meaningless," "Grow, evolve, and make money!" and "No career without excellence." The postmodern heroes of this neoconservatism are those who win on Wall Street, the bankers who are able to write books with titles like *In Praise of Benefits* or *Secrets of Success.*

- *Postmodernity of resistance* would be a vast movement of "deconstruction" led by the rejection of any ideal of fundamental principles or any desire of an overall worldview and governed by intellectual, existential doubt. The emphasis is put on pluralism, decentralization, respect for differences, for what is happening now, breaking with the past, indetermination, and experimentation. Those who express this postmodern current are still "rebels with a cause," some of whom voice their opposition by phrases like "Rather than uniformity, differentiation," "Instead of absolute values, many little gods," "Not production, but communication," and "Instead of final commitments, conditional agreements."

- *Postmodernity of disillusionment* stresses the motives for this disenchantment. Reason, which had been so exalted at first, did not open to the truth, but simply to knowledge for the purpose of dominating others. Progress led to regression since it did not respect humanity and nature. Equality has been based on arbitrary agreements that are broken according to the whim of the moment. The promised happiness is slow in coming, and what we have is full of unhappiness. Most of those belonging to this current of postmodernity are "disgusted rebels." One of them expressed it this way: "In the world in which we live, there is only one thing that I really want: my next vacation." Another one smiled and said:

"Goddess Reason is looking for me, but I can run faster than she can." A third one sang: "Yesterday, yoga, tarot, and meditation. Today, alcohol and drugs. Tomorrow, aerobics and reincarnation."

Change of Era

We are all aware that we are not only in an era of change but also in a change of era. By its very nature, living in such a change of era is a complex affair, a process with an unknown destination, unforeseeable stopping points, and no given timetable, but this moment of historical transition explains why the culture at the beginning of this new millennium is a culture in transition. Our era marks the consummation of cultural modernity and the passage to . . . what we still do not know!

Perhaps we can describe the present cultural situation of the North Atlantic—which influences the rest of the world in differing degrees of intensity—as being a combination of *radical modernity* in the scientific and technological sphere and *postmodernity*, without any defined goal, in the social, family, and interpersonal sphere.

As human beings—and monks and nuns are no exception—we all live, decide, and act from a determined cultural universe. And every change in the cultural universe, in its turn, causes changes of behavior due to new perceptions of reality. The mass media of social communication have created a "cultural industry" based on negotiating with symbols, values, and meanings that change the ways we perceive ourselves and how we relate to ourselves, to others, to the supreme Other, and to other things.

Like every era of transition, ours is an era of crisis. We are living at a critical moment, like the one experienced in the Christian West during the fourteenth and fifteenth centuries. The age of the Renaissance was simultaneously the death of the Middle Ages and the dawn of the modern world. So we are living at a critical juncture, which is open to a new birth but is marked at this time by a crisis of

- *life*: moving from an absolute and sacred conception of reality toward another conception more in terms of some "purely biological phenomenon";

? • *identity*: moving from an old, closed approach toward a different one more open to a process of growth;

- *sexuality*: moving from a genetically and biologically determined conception toward a personal and cultural one with the possibility of its being scientifically chosen;

- *ideology*: moving from an ideal of "organizing life's meaning" toward a rejection of any ideal other than that of "feeling good";

- *meaning*: moving from signs that have lost their authenticity toward signs that are true, or at least that supposedly represent the truth;

- *time*: moving from helping to "use time well" toward teaching to "lose time well";

- *paradigms*: moving from great "frames of reference" toward partial frames of reference;

- *humanity*: moving from a masculine, cerebral, or rational humanity toward a feminine, cordial, and affectionate humanity.

Thirsting for Mystery

From the religious point of view, we are also experiencing a significant transitional crisis. For the sake of extreme simplicity, we can say that modern culture has or has had a pathological conception of religion. For some representatives of modernity, religion was

- a human disease (Nietzsche),

- a social disease (Marx),

- a psychological disease (Freud).

How can we not recall here the Freudian approach to religion and, by extension, to spiritual, religious, and mystical experience? Freud's approach has marked our contemporary world. Religion would be the desire for the protection offered in one's infancy by the father and projected onto an illusory God, since there is no other reality available. Mystics, therefore, downgrade reality, see the world upside down, and, as a consequence of their frustration, submit themselves unconditionally to the suffering this involves. In other words, they are underdeveloped because of the infantile psychosis they are suffering from.

As we have said, modern culture is fragmented, which means that politics, economics, science, the fine arts, and ethics are not influenced by any religious orientation, as was the case in premodern culture. Each particular aspect of culture has freed itself from the religious sphere, is autonomous, obeys its own rules, and organizes itself accordingly. Of itself, this fact should not necessarily contradict religion, but it has favored the development of certain habitual currents of thought that question religion's validity. Examples of these are the tendency to relativize values, to absolutize the exact sciences, to deify the individual ego, and to reject or ignore God as the supreme giver of meaning to reality. We should also remember how certain spokespersons of modern culture proclaimed different forms of God's vanishing:

- God has died: the death of God.

- God keeps silent: the silence of God.

- God is an ideology, either socialist or capitalist: the impersonality of God.

- God is progress: so if he exists, it is only for those in regression!

- God does not exist: so we are the holy ones!

- God is a game: so let's play God!

But religion and mysticism are profoundly human realities, and to deny them would mean stripping humanity of its most basic, transcendent inheritance. This, in fact, has been perceived in recent years by many knowledgeable critics and scientists who understand that, in the presence of what simply exists, language must become silent; that when one touches the inexpressible, one crosses the threshold into mysticism; and when one is in ecstasy, there are no questions and therefore no answers. It is in this context that we can understand the words of Albert Einstein: "Cosmic religious feeling is the strongest and noblest motive for scientific research."[2]

History shows that every period of cultural crisis is a time of religious awakening. When the chain of history and culture is broken or threatens to break, it is religion that returns to reunite the links in the chain. But even though this is a fact, we can still ask why. The fact is that religion has always confronted the great human questions and has tried to reply to them. Where do we come from and where are we going? What exists after death? Who are we and who is God? How can we relate with what is transcendent? Now, if mysticism is the heart of all religions, since it is the experience that generates them, it is clear that every cultural crisis or transition implies a return to mysticism. It is this that explains today's proliferation of mystical offerings in the religious and cultural marketplace.

So now, in the context of postmodern culture, it appears that religion is the best of therapies. Religiosity, instead of being relegated to a far corner of the room, is now obscurely present everywhere, and the nonexisting God has been multiplied into an infinite number of little gods.

In postmodern thinking, we find the appearance of mystery and mysticism, though accompanied by a deinstitutionalization of religion. What are the causes behind this? There are many possible explanations:

- recovery of humanity's traditional mystical heritage

---

[2] "Religion and Science," in *New York Times Magazine* (Nov. 9, 1930) 4; later published in A. Einstein, *The World as I See It* (New York: Philosophical Library, 1949) 28.

- fruit of the meeting between Western culture and Eastern cultures

- sated disgust with the dictatorship of reason

- need for mystery in the face of the scientific pretension to explain everything

- need for austerity and gratuity in the face of the monopoly of efficiency, consumerism, wasted resources, and abuses of nature (Mother Earth) and environment

- fear and trembling at the human ability to transform nature by genetic engineering and atomic science, but its inability to control the consequences of such a transformation

These different causes have given rise to various "mystical" or even "deifying" currents, such as the ecological movement, the growth of sects, the esoteric current, and a more general eclectic tendency. Other forms of sacralized secularity could be added to the list: the sacralization of one's country or race; the worship of and fascination for musical experience, as in rock concerts; the weekend football liturgy; the uncovering of the sacred sanctuary of one's own body. All of this is telling us that the process of de-sacralization is concomitant with another process that sacralizes nature and the world. These two processes show their different faces according to each geographic context and local culture. It is hardly necessary to mention the ambiguity that reigns in all of it.

In this new postmodern cultural context, it is easier to understand and accept the fact that a clinical experience of depth psychology cannot determine what type of beings exist or do not exist. Modern reasoning now admits that jumping from philosophy to theology, from experimental knowledge to the higher levels of being, from physics to metaphysics, or from psychology to spirituality is a serious methodological error. As a young psychiatrist has said: "It is a shame that Freud did not have the chance to psychoanalyze any authentic mystic, and also too bad that he is not alive today in order to help all these stupid and false mystifiers!"

Another way to judge this whole scenario is to speak of a "time of credulity." In this sense we can describe the present North Atlantic culture by pointing to

- the emergence of fundamentalist religiosity, not only among Muslims but also within other major religious traditions; in Christianity there is a religiosity that mixes an updated traditionalism with modern technology, scientific sophistication, and democracy—this is especially evident in the American Evangelical Churches;

- the presence of a movement characterized by a mixture of neo-Gnostic, neomystic, and neoesoteric elements, combining occult secrets with ultramodern applications of physiotherapy, psychotherapy, and ecology without omitting amulets, angels, reincarnation, and karma;

- a sudden awakening of popular religiosity, especially strong and new in Europe, which signifies a mixture of cultural, religious, and traditional elements along with a dose of folklore. Although its followers lack a true catechetical formation in Christian living, this phenomenon, if well directed, could give new life to Christian experience.

Everything seems to show that the North Atlantic culture of the West, branded now by postmodernism, is thirsting for mystery, fed up with ideologies, moralizations, dogmatisms, and ritualisms. This cultural context lets us return to a new esteem for genuine religious and mystical experience. Our faith needs the experience of conversion and prayer so that it can produce a theology that respects mystery, knowing that all our knowledge, in the presence of the Mystery, is but an approximation, and all our speaking, mere babbling.

Besides, "the new attention paid by the various cultural currents of our time to religious experience, and to Christianity in particular, spurs us to persevere on the path we have chosen towards a fresh meeting between the Gospel and culture."[3] So,

---

[3] John Paul II, general audience, November 25, 1998.

while being careful not to fall into a mystical fideism and its more sentimental heresies, we "are in duty bound to offer a generous welcome and spiritual support to all those who, moved by a thirst for God and a desire to live the demands of faith, turn to [us]."[4]

[4] John Paul II, *Vita Consecrata*, 103.

Chapter 2

Our Life's Purpose

Here is how Bernard of Clairvaux describes the calling of monks and nuns: "In the Church the 'bed' where one reposes [*quiescitur*] is, in my opinion, the cloisters and monasteries, where one lives undisturbed [*quiete*] by the cares of the world and the anxieties of life."[1]

This is the common teaching of all our early Cistercian Fathers. They may change metaphors and words, but the content remains the same. William of Saint-Thierry and Isaac of Stella put it this way:

> It is for others to serve God, it is for you to cling to him; it is for others to believe in God, know him, love him and revere him; it is for you to taste him, understand him, be acquainted with him, enjoy him.[2]

> Joy, love, delight, sight, sweetness, light and glory—these are what God asks of us, the purpose for which he made us. To do what we were created to do, this is right order and true religion. Let us make sovereign Beauty our contemplation, set our hearts on highest Delight, be ruthless against whatever hinders such sight and enjoyment. All our observances, our work and leisure, our speech and silence, all must be directed to such contemplation.[3]

---

[1] Saint Bernard, *On the Song of Songs* 46.2.
[2] William of Saint-Thierry, *The Golden Epistle*, I:v, 15.
[3] Isaac of Stella, *Sermons* 25.7.

Present Relevance

We can wonder, however, whether this teaching is still valid and useful today. It doubtlessly is, provided we are realistic and live it prudently. I will let one of my predecessors as abbot general explain what our approach should be. I refer to Dom Gabriel Sortais in one of his exhortations to the Order:

> Would that God would implant in each and every member of the Order the conviction that each is called to pursue a life of contemplation! That is the all-in-all of the Cistercian. It is by contemplation that we glorify God, that we achieve holiness, that we concur with Jesus in the sanctification of souls.[4]

It is easy to see that Dom Gabriel is asking for the grace to persuade all the members of the Order about the meaning of the Cistercian vocation, which is a clear sign that, at least in practice, not everyone is so convinced. Here is what another abbot general, Dom Ignace Gillet, has to say for his part:

> Often the Abbot General is asked: "Are there real contemplatives in the Order, and are there many of them?" I think that there are two answers to this and that they come near to contradicting one another. Yes: there are true contemplatives in the Order, and more than you think. It is equally certain that there are far fewer than one would wish. If there is anyone who, the darkness notwithstanding, perseveres with faith in this search for God, he is a true contemplative. That is what I mean when I say that there are many contemplatives in the Order. Probably it is because we are not ready enough for renunciation that we are so little contemplative. For us, too, it is because we fail to go the whole way in self-renunciation that so many in our communities are half-baked contemplatives.[5]

---

[4] G. Sortais, circular letter of December 8, 1951. See also his circular letter of June 16, 1961.
[5] I. Gillet, circular letter of January 6, 1970. See also his circular letters of 1971 and 1972.

Yet another abbot general, Dom Ambrose Southey, in his day invited us to "build up the contemplative aspect of our life."[6] He took up this theme again from another angle in a conference to the General Chapter of 1984, when he said: "If there are few men of deep prayer, it is because few are ready to seek God by this road of facing our own reality and that of God." In practice, he continued, this road consists in "overcoming our self-love, accepting an authentic solitude, and finding our identity in Christ."[7]

In principle, therefore, and in the official statements of the Order, we can still say that "our life is entirely oriented toward the experience of the living God"[8] and that "Our Order is a monastic institute wholly ordered to contemplation."[9]

Actions, of course, speak louder than words, which is the reason why I have, from the beginning of my service as abbot general, invited all the members of the Order to take a new step along the road of renewal. And a basic feature of this renewal is its *orientation toward the Mystery, under the guidance of the Cistercian mystics*.

Cistercian Teachers of Mysticism

The Fathers of Cîteaux are not only mystics but also *mystagogues*—that is, teachers who introduce their listeners to the Mystery of God and to the hidden depths of the human spirit. They enter into the Mystery so that we, too, can enter, and they do not hide their experience when it could be helpful for others. As good teachers, they are ready for anything: "I am telling you of what comes within my own experience. Whenever I discover that any of you have benefited from my admonitions, then I confess that I never regret preferring the preparation of my sermon to my personal leisure and quietude."[10]

---

[6] A. Southey, circular letter of 1980. See also his opening conference at the General Chapter of 1980.

[7] Minutes of the General Chapter of 1984 (Rome), appendix I (11–12).

[8] "Declaration on Cistercian Life," in Minutes of the Sessions of the General Chapter of 1969 (Rome) 275.

[9] *Constitutions OCSO*, 2.

[10] Bernard, *Song* 51.3.

When we speak of observances, vices, or sin, we know what we are talking about and do not need others to explain what we are saying; but when we speak about mysticism, it is usually a different story. The subject is too big for us and we need guides. The only road that will take us beyond what we usually experience is that of a disciple's docility to the teaching of a master. That is why we have to turn to Christian mystics—in order to be taught by them. And even beyond them, we need to have recourse to the entire heritage of Christian mysticism, since any single person, no matter how holy he or she may be, cannot exhaust either the Mystery or the mystical experience of the Mystery.

The writings of the mystics flow from their experience of God and his Mystery, which is why these writings contain and communicate a spiritual experience. Entering into these texts involves touching this experience and letting ourselves be touched by it. In other words, the writings of the mystics are channels between them and us, and the witness of their experience will somehow stimulate a similar experience in our own heart. When they write, the mystics are not just telling us about the Mystery but are, above all, introducing us into it. In the same way that a mystic "suffers" in himself what is divine, so his or her writings are destined to "startle" us. In a mysterious way, such mystical writings submerge us in the Mystery.

Perhaps a comparison with poetry can help. Both poetry and music are fruits of an experience of beauty and attempt to awaken a similar experience in the reader or listener. We all have some experience of beauty, which explains why poetry and music can enkindle such an experience in us. In the same way, we all have been created in the image of God and are invited to enter into the divine Mystery. In fact, we already have some experience of God, so that the writings of the mystics wake up this divine vocation in us by attracting us to the Mystery and giving us reasons to practice charity, which confirms the authenticity of our new awareness and attraction.

It could be said that the words in mystical writings are not spoken words but words speaking now to the reader—that is, living words, writings that live and speak. This is why they often seem discontinuous, with a certain lack of clear logic that is typical of live conversation and needs to be completed with the emotion and love that remain unexpressed.

Finally, let me point out an analogy between the writings of the mystics and Sacred Scripture. The latter contains and communicates the experience of God's salvation, mediating to us this experience of being saved. Our *lectio divina* is meant to take us beyond the words of the text we read so as to experience the Person of the Lord. Without exaggerating the comparison, we can say something similar about the writings of the mystics. If the biblical authors wrote in the Spirit, mystical authors have written in the spirit of the Spirit.

Medieval Mystagogues

Ladies first. It is evident that the feminine mentality of our medieval mystical sisters—I am thinking of Lutgarde, Hadewijch, Beatrice, Mechtild, Gertrude, and others—is more inclined to creative imagination than to creative thought. There is a big difference between these. Creative thought functions on the level of ideas and concepts, whereas creative imagination is based on intuition, feeling, and fantasy. Here it is a question not of thinking but of dreaming wide awake and creatively. Scripture offers us a good example of this, since there we meet a God who reveals himself more by the symbols and images of art than by the conceptual ideas of modern science. Creative imagination makes room for a metaphorical theology that starts from an experience and then communicates its message by recreating that experience through more lengthy narratives and historical reenactments.

The visions and revelations of our mystical sisters should be interpreted this way and not through any kind of rational or scientific hermeneutics. Their language of desire and love is a language of the affective imagination. What they say is always less than what they want, which explains why what they say always carries with it a certain emptiness, a lack. The interpretation of a mystical vision has something in common with the interpretation of a painting, a musical composition, or a literary or poetic work of art, where the only valid approach is an aesthetic one. If people do not think this is true, let them read or interpret rationally, for example, the vocational vision of the prophet Jeremiah in Jeremiah 1:4-19, or the visions of the book of Revelation. Then we will see where they end up.

It would be good to explain a little more carefully here some of the mystical visions coming from so many medieval women. Theological anthropology distinguishes three types of perception when it comes to "visions": visions by the exterior senses, interior visions thanks to the "interior senses," and spiritual visions. It is clear that in the visions of the mystics we are referring to, there is no question of the normal exterior perception of the five senses. In other words, the images and figures they see do not exist exteriorly or spatially. Neither is it a question of "intellectual visions" without any images, such as can occur in other mystical experiences. It is rather a question of the intermediate category, that of interior perceptions, which can certainly have the force, for the visionary herself, of a presence equivalent to an external stimulus of the senses.

Seeing interiorly does not mean imagining subjectively, but rather that the soul is affected by something real, although above the senses, and is able to see what is not perceived by the senses, through a type of vision by the "interior senses." The objects of this vision are true objects, which touch the soul, but they do not belong to our habitual world of sense knowledge. To arrive at this, an interior vigilance of heart is required, which most persons do not have because of the strong pressure from external realities and from images and thoughts that fill the soul. In an interior vision, the person is carried beyond mere exteriority so that other deeper dimensions of reality touch her and become visible to her.

An interior vision has its limitations. Even in an exterior vision a subjective factor is always present because we see not only the object but also whatever comes to us through the filter of our senses, which have to carry out a process of translation. This is even more evident in an interior vision, especially when it is a question of realities that of themselves surpass our limited horizon of experience. The subject, the visionary, is involved even more intimately in all of this. She sees according to the modes of knowledge and symbolism available to her. In such an interior vision, there is a wider process of translation than for an external vision, so that the visionary becomes essentially a sharer in the formation of the image of what is revealed to her. Such visions are never simply "photographs" of what is beyond the senses, but also contain within themselves the possibilities and limitations of the perceiving subject.

The images thus produced are, as it were, a synthesis of the impulse coming from on high and the possibilities at the disposal of the perceiving subject. That is why the imaginative language of these visions is symbolic. Our mystics, therefore, are theologians, but not scholastic ones. Rather, they are experiential theologians. Their theology is an incarnated theology in continuity with the Mystery of the incarnation, which is why we can speak of a femininely sexualized theology in which the bodily, affective, and imaginative aspects play an important part.

This is the only way we are going to understand the spousal mysticism that is such an outstanding feature of these mystical women. Their experiences are rooted in their affective life and, more specifically, in that zone where the union of the human couple is expressed most sexually and physically. The Bible, once again, with its Song of Songs and its Prophets, puts us on this same wavelength.

Our Cistercian mystagogues received the charism of "the utterance of wisdom," mentioned by Saint Paul in his first letter to the Corinthians.[11] This gratuitous gift from the Lord is for teaching in a way that will capture, persuade, and enlighten the intellect, move the affections, order the will, and unite it to what is good and to the truth. Many of these men and women already had a natural gift for speaking and writing, but the Spirit added to this the *utterance of wisdom*.

[11] 1 Cor 12:8.

If, after nine centuries of history, we still exist today, it is because our early Cistercian Fathers and Mothers had, in differing degrees,

- a capacity for theological transcendence, which they had experienced in a full and complete way—that is to say, a mystical way—so that they might be a model for future generations;

- a striking gift of reflecting on their lived experience in all its dimensions, and the art of initiating others in the same experience;

- a notable skill in putting this experience down in writing and in creating communities and groups that would transmit this transcendent heritage of mystical theology.

The mystical dimension of our life is extremely important for orienting—or reorienting—our lives. If we lose sight of it, we run the risk of wandering down the wrong path. We should never hesitate to tell our candidates most clearly that our life is open to, and has as its goal, the mystical dimension of Christian life. We cannot doubt that the one thing that gives meaning to our monastic life is the personal, experiential encounter with Christ Jesus.

Chapter 3

Initial Clarifications

Now a word about mystery, mysticism, mystics, and the mystical experience. All these realities are intimately bound together. We distinguish them in order to make them more easily understood, but we will see clearly that it is not possible to speak of one of them without referring to the others.

Mystery

The "mystery" we are talking about is not a synonym for an enigma or a problem, as in a "mystery story." Mystery is incomprehensible, but not unintelligible. If it were unintelligible, it would be absurd. Mystery refers to the deepest dimension of reality, to the final nucleus that gives meaning to everything that exists. This is why each and every human being is a mystery and has been created for living this mystery. Human intelligence and human love are able to incorporate this mystery, even though sin so often urges human reasoning to pretend to block it out.

The human person, being intelligent and free, is programmed from within, in an indelible way, to tend toward mystery. This orientation, which springs from the most hidden roots of our being, is precisely what makes each one of us a person.

Men and women of every age and place tell us that mystery is diffused throughout nature, and so they talk about "something really special." Artists and poets go even further and intuit the fact that this *something special* enchanting and seducing them surpasses any sensory or reasonable beauty. Philosophers, for

their part, know that in the depths of all being there is something
that has always been known, yet always remains *unknown*.

Anthropology of all centuries tells us that the human person
need not go far from his or her inner self to find mystery. Traditional religions speak of "the totally Other" to designate mystery,
but what we are now interested in is what the Bible, especially
the New Testament, means by "mystery."

The pagan mystery cults are, strictly speaking, "those secret
religious rites believed to impart enduring bliss to the initiate."[1]
In the hermetism of second- and third-century Alexandria, the
term began to be applied to a religious philosophy. In a strictly
Christian context, however, Saint Paul uses the word "mystery"
in a doctrinal and religious sense, more influenced by Jewish
wisdom literature and its apocalyptic writings, which were far
from the influence of any Greek religious philosophy. For Paul,
the Mystery is *the divine plan*—hidden at the beginning, then
revealed—to establish a relationship between God and the
human family in Christ.[2]

The communion of all persons with God, their relation of
divine adoption as children of God, is accomplished in Christ.
Christ is the mediator because he is "Christ in you, the hope of
glory,"[3] incorporating the Church into himself as "his own
body."[4] In other words, it is a divine project of becoming children
of God and members of one and the same divine family: "Those
whom he foreknew he also predestined to be conformed to the
image of his Son, in order that he might be the firstborn within
a large family."[5]

This Mystery is revealed and fulfilled in the Church. It is
known by Christians and lived by them in many ways, the chief
one being the interior experience given by the Holy Spirit. It is

---

[1] *Merriam-Webster's Collegiate Dictionary*, 11th ed. (2008), s.v. "mystery."
[2] Cf. Eph 3:8-9.
[3] Col 1:27.
[4] Col 1:24.
[5] Rom 8:29.

in this sense that Paul speaks of "knowledge and full insight."[6] Basically, it is a question of an experience of the Spirit that interiorly transforms believers by letting Christ dwell in their human heart, rooting them in love.[7]

The best Pauline text on the Mystery describes it this way: "He [God the Father] has made known to us the mystery of his will, according to his good pleasure that he set forth in Christ, as a plan for the fullness of time, to gather up all things in him, things in heaven and things on earth."[8] Christian mysticism must always be understood in terms of this Mystery.

Jesus' whole life—not only his incarnation, death, and resurrection—is Mystery. His very humanity is a sign of his divinity since the visibility of his earthly life leads to the hidden, invisible Mystery of his divine sonship and universal mission of salvation.

During his public life, Jesus himself told his followers: "To you it has been given to know the secrets of the kingdom of heaven."[9] This revelation, moreover, caused him great joy:

> I thank you, Father, Lord of heaven and earth, because you have hidden these things from the wise and the intelligent and have revealed them to infants; yes, Father, for such was your gracious will. All things have been handed over to me by my Father; and no one knows the Son except the Father, and no one knows the Father except the Son and anyone to whom the Son chooses to reveal him.[10]

The Fathers of the Church took up in different ways Saint Paul's concept of the Mystery. We can say synthetically that the Mystery is the divine plan of salvation in Christ through the Spirit. Its principal features, as a hidden design that has now been revealed, are that it is

---

[6] Phil 1:9. Also Eph 1:15-19; Col 1:3-5, 9-12; 2:2-3; 3:39-14; 2 Cor 2:6-10.
[7] See Eph 3:16-17.
[8] Eph 1:9-10. See the entire hymn of Eph 1 and Col 1:25-26.
[9] Mt 13:11 and parallels.
[10] Mt 11:25-27 and parallels.

- *eternal*, because God conceived it from the beginning and forever;

- *free*, springing from the totally free decision of the divine will;

- *intelligent*, since it is the fruit of infinite, divine wisdom;

- *loving*, because love is what the Mystery contains and exists for;

- *historical*, continually appearing and making itself present in time and space;

- *personal*, addressing each particular individual as a unique and unrepeatable being;

- *communitarian*, since it embraces everyone in a fraternal, ecclesial relation of love;

- *up to date*, because it points to "now" in the life of each one of us;

- *liturgical*, so that it can be celebrated and actively shared through meaningful symbols;

- *irrevocable*, because God does not repent or take back his given word;

- *transcendent*, always surpassing our ability to understand it;

- *in Christ*, so that the mystery of man is clarified in the mystery of the incarnate, crucified, and risen Word.

Now, we can ask what the Christian Mystery basically consists of. The answer is that, strictly speaking, there are only three mysteries that are totally *original*, in the sense that all other mysteries flow from them: the mystery of the Most Holy Trinity; the mystery of the redemptive incarnation, death, and resurrection of God's eternal Son; and the mystery of the divinization of human beings by grace. All other truths of the faith are mysteries insofar as they are related to these original mysteries. A result of this is that mystical experience is primarily related to these fundamental mysteries and, through them, to the other mysteries, all of them finding their fulfillment and point of convergence in the Risen Christ.

We can now say that the "Mystery of faith" contains, in summary form, all that Christian life and existence is. "The Church professes this mystery in the Apostles' Creed and celebrates it in the sacramental liturgy, so that the life of the faithful may be conformed to Christ in the Holy Spirit to the glory of God the Father. This mystery, then, requires that the faithful believe in it, that they celebrate it, and that they live from it in a vital and personal relationship with the living and true God. This relationship is prayer." [11] In the light of this, we can better understand the other affirmation in the *Catechism:* "Spiritual progress tends toward ever more intimate union with Christ. This union is called 'mystical' because it participates in the mystery of Christ through the sacraments—'the holy mysteries'—and, in him, in the mystery of the Holy Trinity. God calls us all to this intimate union with him, even if the special graces or extraordinary signs of this mystical life are granted only to some for the sake of manifesting the gratuitous gift given to all." [12]

I think it is important to have it clear that mystery and mysticism are characterized by a globally unifying power. Through ignorance or lack of experience we often associate mystical realities with something "different" that thus becomes a cause of separation, and this at different levels:

- separation from what is reasonable, because mystery and things mystical offer access to truths unattainable to human intelligence

- separation from the secular world, since they only take place in the realm of the sacred

- separation from the body, for mystery and things mystical only have to do with the spirit

---

[11] *Catechism of the Catholic Church,* n. 2558.
[12] *Catechism of the Catholic Church,* n. 2014.

- separation from the community, because they only take place in the individual heart

- separation from history, since they are pointing to eternity

Such a "separatist" approach to mystery and mysticism seems to forget that it is not religion that binds us to God but rather something else that makes such a bond possible: "[God] is not far from each one of us. For in him we live and move and have our being."[13]

Mysticism

Mysticism is a human reality that is not limited to any religion. It is the climax of the encounter between Absolute Being and the human being. There have been mystics everywhere and at all times. Because of the fact that the human being has been created in the image of God, it is not strange if we think and say that the deepest center of the human soul is capable, under certain conditions, to experience something of the divine presence, even though reason does not understand what is happening.

That is what explains why Vatican II says that "the root reason for human dignity lies in man's call to communion with God. From the very circumstance of his origin man is already invited to converse with God. For man would not exist were he not created by God's love and constantly preserved by it."[14] The mystical aspiration, therefore, is something inherent to human nature. Every human being comes from one and the same Creator, so that human nature in its deepest reality is always the same. It is always created in the image of God and tends toward the perfection of its likeness to him.

Prior to Christianity, the word "mystical" was used in ancient Greece to refer not so much to an arcane doctrine as to a *ritual* secret. When the term passed into Christianity, it acquired a doctrinal and experiential connotation, so that understanding it requires

[13] Acts 17:27-28.
[14] *Gaudium et Spes*, n. 19.

understanding at the same time what the term "mystery" means. The whole purpose of the "mystery" is for it to be revealed and then received through knowledge and love. The degrees of its reception will depend on the light and fire given by the Spirit and on the dispositions of the human receivers. Revelation and faith constitute the mystery of the meeting between God and humanity in Christ Jesus:

> In His goodness and wisdom God chose to reveal Himself and to make known to us the hidden purpose of His will by which through Christ, the Word made flesh, man might in the Holy Spirit have access to the Father and come to share in the divine nature.[15]

The process of this human appropriation of the divine mystery advances from the simple act of believing on to the mysterious experience of something "mystical"; but all are called to grow at every stage of this process. Paul the apostle offers up his struggles for the Christians of Colossus "so that they may have all the riches of assured understanding and have the knowledge of God's mystery, that is, Christ himself, in whom are hidden all the treasures of wisdom and knowledge."[16]

We recall in this context Jesus' question to his disciples and the dialogue that followed: " 'But who do you say that I am?' Simon Peter answered, 'You are the Messiah, the Son of the living God.' And Jesus answered him, 'Blessed are you, Simon son of Jonah! For flesh and blood has not revealed this to you, but my Father in heaven.' "[17]

It is true that the word "mystical" does not occur in the Bible, but what we mean by it can be clarified by going back to Scripture, since the mystical element is far from absent from it. In fact, Sacred Scripture speaks in many and various ways about how God relates to human beings and how they share in the living Mystery of God.

---

[15] *Dei Verbum*, n. 2.
[16] Col 2:2-3.
[17] Mt 16:15-17.

First and foremost, there is the proclamation that, prior to any human interest in God, it was God who was concerned about us.[18] God is the first one to break the silence with his creating word.[19] He is "at the door, knocking,"[20] and Paul, quoting the prophet Isaiah, has the Lord say: "I have been found by those who did not seek me."[21]

The "mystical" teaching of the Bible states that the human being is known and loved by God before he or she knows or loves God.[22] Scripture constantly affirms the primacy of divine revelation over any human search for it and the similar primacy of grace over merit. That is why God's kingdom grows like the seed in the earth, even though the farmer is asleep.[23] In other words, divine "good will"[24] always precedes the human will, good or bad.

This God, who is always ahead of us and comes out of himself to meet us, is principally revealed

- in salvation history, as witnessed by Israel's basic creed[25] and Christian belief in the incarnation, which sees God's supreme revelation and perfect sanctuary in the flesh of Christ;[26]

- in the cosmic temple of creation[27] or the temple of Mount Sion;[28]

- in his efficacious Word, which makes the dry earth of human existence fertile.[29]

---

[18] See Is 40:27; 49:14-16.
[19] See Gen 1.
[20] Rev 3:20.
[21] Rom 10:20.
[22] See Gal 4:9.
[23] See Mk 4:26-29.
[24] Lk 2:14.
[25] See Dt 26:6-9; Ps 135(136); Jos 24:1-13.
[26] See Jn 1:14; 2:19-22; 1 Cor 6:19.
[27] See Ps 18(19); 103(104).
[28] See 1 Kgs 8.
[29] See Is 55:10-11.

The second basic statement of the Bible about mysticism is this: *Immanû-ᵓel,* "God-with-us," demands to have a free, loving dialogue with the people he creates. God gives himself so that the person he has created will receive him. Christ calls us at the door and speaks; the believer has to open up to him and reply.

Scripture uses three fundamental categories when it presents this dialogue of self-gift and reception, of calling and answering. The first category is that of agape. It is clear that God takes the initiative here.[30] The human person responds in two directions at once, vertically to God and horizontally to his neighbor.[31] It is precisely the horizontal direction that serves to verify the authenticity of the mystical experience, which at its height makes the believer love as God does.[32] This category of agape involves a rich ensemble of symbols:

- *paternal* symbols, like the loving care and education of a child through purifying trials[33]

- *maternal* symbols, expressing the intense tenderness in a meeting of total trust[34]

- *spousal* symbols, reflecting the experience of human love between man and woman[35]

The second category is *communion* and refers to *dwelling* and *abiding,* as presented by John the evangelist in the Lord's words at the Last Supper[36] and in the First Letter of John.[37] It extends to the symbols of the vine and the branches[38] and the Bread of Life.[39]

---

[30] See 1 Jn 4:10, 19; Eph 2:4.
[31] See Mt 22:37; Dt 6:5; Jn 15:12.
[32] See 1 Cor 13; Mt 5:48.
[33] See Dt 8:5; Hos 11:1-4.
[34] See Is 49:15; Ps 130(131); Lk 15.
[35] See Hos 1–3; Is 54; 62:1-5; Jer 2:2; Ez 16; Song, passim.
[36] See Jn 13:17.
[37] See 1 Jn 1:7; 3:16; 4:7, 11, 16, 20-21.
[38] See Jn 15:1-6.
[39] See Jn 6:32-58.

The third category is that of *life* and is the broadest one since it allows God to "be all in all."[40] It unfolds in different forms:

- *a new covenant* that implies the infusion of the divine Spirit and a change of heart[41]

- *belonging*, according to the words of the psalmist: "Save me, for I am yours,"[42] and even more those of Saint Paul: "To me, living is Christ"; "And it is no longer I who live, but it is Christ who lives in me"; "[Our] life is hidden with Christ in God"[43]

- *eternity*, since mystical life never ends, being divine life itself;[44] the Christian who has shared in Christ's Passover will live forever with the Lord,[45] and nothing can separate him from that love, the love of his God[46]

The teaching of the Church Fathers on mysticism is also somewhat complex, and we do not need to develop it here. The patristic texts crystallizing around the concept *mystikós* make references to four interrelated dimensions:

- the *mystical-biblical dimension*, in which the reference is to the allegorical meaning of Scripture, in which ultimately the key and only real meaning is Christ

- the *mystical-liturgical dimension*, where the reality of mystery is simultaneously the content of Scripture and of the sacraments during the eucharistic celebration

- the *mystical-spiritual dimension*, which refers to a direct, almost experiential way of knowing God through deep communion with him

---

[40] 1 Cor 15:28.
[41] See Jer 31:31-34; Ez 36:24-27.
[42] Ps 118(119):94.
[43] Phil 1:21; Gal 2:20; Col 3:3.
[44] Ps 15(16):2, 10-11; 72(73):23-28.
[45] See Gal 6:17; 1 Thess 4:17.
[46] See Rom 8:35-39.

- the *mystical-divinizing dimension*, which is the mystery contemplated in the Scriptures, celebrated in the liturgy, and
fulfilled in Christians as their divinization is achieved

In these almost two thousand years of Christian history, we
observe a triple use of the terms "mystic" or "mysticism," so that
we can talk about its purely objective use, its objective-subjective
use, and its purely subjective use:

- *Objective use*, which was predominant during the first four
Christian centuries. What is hidden (*mystikós* or *mystérion*)
is found and revealed in Scripture's mystical or christologi-
cal sense (Origen) and in the liturgical celebration of baptism, with its mystical regeneration in Christ (Saint Nilus,
Eusebius), and of the Eucharist, the mystical sacrifice of
Christ (apostolic constitutions).

- *Objective-subjective use*, which was the usual one in the
twelfth century. Revelation is not seen as a series of truths
external to the human person, but rather as life transforming
and as fulfilling the person by satisfying the deepest desires
of the human heart. Personal experience was always subor-
dinated to the objectivity of what has been revealed: "Put
your trust, therefore, in the judgment of faith and not in your
own experience,"[47] especially when prayer is unanswered,
because "I hold fast by faith what I cannot grasp with my
mind."[48] Mysticism is therefore a reality of grace accompanying the entire life of the believer as it transforms the person
from dawn into midday and from burning coals into fire.

- *Subjective use*, which has predominated since the fifteenth
century. This could refer to a *common* and deeply lived experience of, or encounter with, the Mystery. Or it could refer
to a *special* experience of the Mystery, with affective awareness of its presence through a loving knowledge, fruit of an
especially infused gift from God. Some elements of this

[47] Bernard, *Sermons for Lent* 5.5.
[48] Bernard, *Song* 76.6.

experience are the divine action making it possible; the new light of knowledge and fire of love; an active "passivity"; a mediated immediacy; intuition of the Presence; union and reciprocal communication.

It is worth repeating something often said in different ways—namely, that Christian mysticism is the fulfillment of the Mystery of Christ in us. That is why it has to be emphasized that the Mystery and its mysticism are not two independent realities that can exist in separation from one another. The single real entity is Mystery-mysticism, *Pléroma*, Fullness—that is, the Mystery at work in us. It is in the full development of the Mystery in us that we find the subjective and objective dimensions of the entire Christian mystical experience. This full development has two aspects: Christ living in us and we living in Christ, all by the will of the Father, in communion with the Son's death and resurrection, through the Spirit's work, and in the Church.

These various aspects of the Mystery explain the differing expressions of mystical experience and can also explain the different features that exist among the mystics. For the time being, what I have said about Christian mysticism would seem to be enough. I will just add a few points to synthesize what has been said and to distinguish Christian mysticism from other forms of mysticism.

Specifically Christian mysticism shows the following characteristics:

- It is a grace, God's gift, not the fruit of human effort. Thus, it presupposes the humility of a subject who is not looking to obtain any particular religious experience, but simply aspires to loving union with God, a harmonious agreement of wills.

- It refers to the Christian mystery, to a particular way of living it. Since it is homogeneous with the mystery, it will never go beyond it.

- It passes through the humanity of Christ, or at least is open to it in such a way that his humanity can be easily found, which implies the paschal dimension of death and life, passion and resurrection, cross and glory.

- There is no separation between spirit and matter, which are two dimensions united by the mysteries of incarnation and resurrection. It is the whole human being who has been redeemed and purified by the death and resurrection of Christ.

- It includes an ecclesial and social dimension, since a mysterious current of grace is generated in mystical union, for the good of the Church and for all humanity.

- It is born, nourished, and fulfilled in the exercise of gospel love.

In other words, Christian mysticism is inseparable from Christianity as an institutional organism, in its liturgical celebration, in its evangelical morality, and as an ongoing tradition of theological reflection.

Mystics

All that has been said so far has helped us understand what and who the mystics are. They are simply all those persons who enter into the Mystery of Christ and are being transformed by it. In this sense, everyone baptized is a mystic, but that does not mean that every baptized person has undergone a mystical experience. In general the mystical experience of most Christians is "latent," still unformed at the level of awareness and the feelings. So we can say that mystical life is wider and more inclusive than mystical experience, the latter being a personal condensation of the wider reality.

A mystic is someone who experiences God's Mystery. Our normal situation is one of living these realities without experiencing them. We live divine grace and the theological virtues, but we do not experience what we live. Likewise in our daily natural life we do not always experience what we are living. Who, for example, experiences breathing, digesting, normal blood circulation, cells multiplying, or fingernails growing?

The great mystics experience the Mystery not only at times but even permanently, each according to his or her condition, as a man, a woman, or an adolescent, according to his or her respective character, temperament, sensitivity, culture, and so forth. In a more particular way, mystics are those people who have experienced the revelation of the Mystery, thanks to a mysterious divine infusion that shows itself through knowledge and love, light, and fire.

Mystical experience is a divine gift that presupposes the theological virtues and the presence of the Holy Spirit with his gifts. The action of the Spirit causes a new, different state of awareness. In the strict and proper sense, a mystic is someone who experiences this action of the Spirit and this different state of consciousness habitually and intensely. In a more temporary form and in lesser degrees of intensity, however, such experiences are much more common than we might think. The so-called inspirations of grace can be counted among such experiences and are certainly known by all Christians trying to be faithful to a serious spiritual life.

Our experience of the mystery—our lived awareness of its presence and communication—is always accompanied by ascetical effort; that is to say, it transforms us behaviorally and unites us with God in mutual love, which is a harmonious agreement of wills.

Mystical Experience

The word "experience" has not always enjoyed good press relations in the Latin Church, even though it has always been held in esteem in Christian Churches of the East. Many Western Christians and theologians seem to have forgotten the traditional Thomistic doctrine of "correct judgment made through empathy or connaturality with divine things."[49] In order to avoid any

---

[49] Thomas Aquinas, *Summa Theologiae*, II-II, 45, 2: *Rectum judicium habere de eis (rebus divinis) secundum quamdam connaturalitatem . . .; compassio sive connaturalitas ad res divinas.*

misunderstanding, I want to begin by what I do *not* mean by the word "experience":

- an *emotional meaning*, which would eliminate any room for freedom and conscientious behavior

- an *experimental meaning*, when you take possession of something to verify some data

- an *unmediated meaning*, which is implicitly saying, "This is it! I am God!"

When I speak of experience, therefore, I am not referring to the above uses of the word. By "experience" I mean a knowledge springing from dwelling in what has been accepted, or an episode or period of an integral human life authenticated as such in a relationship. Applying this to Christian mystical experience, we could say that the latter is a particular element of a fully normal life determined by a relationship with God communicating himself in Christ, or that it is a knowledge springing from faith accepting God's revelation in Christ. This can be further enriched by Saint Thomas's teaching that "this empathy, or connaturality with divine things, results from charity which unites us to God." We are dealing, therefore, with wisdom, a gift of the Holy Spirit that permits the mutual indwelling of the lover and the beloved.[50]

Thus, Christian mystical experience is a modality of faith, a particular way of living faith. It is at the service of faith, is discerned by it, and witnesses to it. It only exists within the faith of the Church, which means that it is connected to the sacramental celebration of faith and to a faith-filled reading of God's Word in the Church.

Starting in the fifteenth century, as we saw, the more subjective aspect came to the forefront in any discussion of Christian mystical experience. From then on, mysticism is spoken of in reference

---

[50] Thomas Aquinas, *Summa Theologiae*, II-II, 45, 2: *Hujusmodi autem compassio sive connaturalitas ad res divinas fit per caritatem, quae quidem unit nos Deo: secundum illud 1 ad Cor. VI, Qui adhaeret Deo unus spiritus est.* See also I, 1, 6, ad 3; I-II, 28, 2.

to personal—that is, affective and conscious—experience of the Mystery through knowledge and love, thanks to a special, divine influence. Its different ingredients are analyzed and emphasized: God's enabling action, the new light of knowledge and love, active passivity, intuition of God's presence, reciprocal union, and communication. These experiences can refer both to the Mystery of the inner life of the triune God and to the Mystery of his saving will, everything reaching us through Christ and in the Spirit.

It is not hard to distinguish different types of experiences within the vast sweep of communication between God and his human children. A simple reading of classical religious literature allows us speak of mystical experience that is

- *essential*: union with God expressed in terms of absorption and "identity" in the depths or essence of the soul—this is the negative or *apophatic* way;

- *spousal*: union or relationship with God expressed as a spousal covenant opening the door to becoming one spirit with God in Christ—this is the affirmative or *cataphatic* way;

- *contemplative*: infused contemplation, loving knowledge, warm light, light-giving flame, hidden presence, inhabited desert, and so forth, with emphasis either on knowledge or love;

- *apostolic*: acting with Christ as he saves the world in history;

- *cosmic*: encounter with God through creation, which reveals or unveils him;

- *interpersonal*: revelation of Christ in the service of one's neighbor and in the love of friendship;

- *ordinary*: presences and absences, consolations and desolations, inspirations and temptation, desire and love in the life of the sincere Christian;

- *accidental*: various phenomena that sometimes accompany the mystical entrance into the Mystery, such as ecstasy, raptures, touches, visions, locutions—this also includes extraordinary or charismatic phenomena, such as prophetic revelations, stigmata, or clairvoyance.

Unfortunately, when we speak of mysticism and mystical experience, we often think and speak of accidental experiences and push entirely to one side what is the living substance. This has occasioned many misunderstandings and fears, which have ended up causing a rejection of mysticism and of many authentic mystics. This does not mean that I wish to discredit the many mystics who undergo these accidental phenomena. My only desire is to affirm clearly that these happenings do not constitute the substance of mysticism. On the other hand, it would be an impoverishment of mysticism not to recognize all that such phenomena teach us about possible approaches to the Mystery and about human nature in its relationship to God.

Mystical experiences fall within the normal development of the life of grace and the growth of the theological virtues. It is in this sense that every baptized person is a mystic, and mystics are not special persons. They experience the same realities that any other Christian does, but they experience them differently. God's grace acts in the mystic just as in any other person, but the mystic knows that it is grace that is working.

It is obvious that there are an infinite number of degrees to the intensity of such experiences. Their intensity will depend on the flow of divine generosity and on the capacity for such an experience on the part of the receiver. They are usually more striking at moments of change or transition, such as a conversion or decision that will govern the future of one's life. In the same way, periods of an intense desert experience make someone more sensitive to God's action. On the other hand, it also has to be said that these experiences often happen without any known cause, although they are helped along by a general climate of sincere, persevering faith, hope, and charity. And they usually lead to a more stable state of soul in which clarity and obscurity are blended together, like a hidden dawn or dusk, in which neither light nor darkness predominates. In any case, these experiences often accompany us throughout our life in the Spirit and play a key role in our process of ongoing conversion, their final purpose being to conform us to the image and likeness of Christ the Lord.

In conclusion, I would like to stress five important features of Christian mystical experience:

- It is not something separate from Christianity as a religion, but rather one of its particular, concrete aspects.

- In the second place, this experience should be considered, above all, as a process or way of life more than as an isolated experience of God.

- Third, this experiential process of fellowship with God is transforming and divinizing.

- In the fourth place, instead of speaking about "mystical experience," it would be better to speak about *experience of the Mystery*.

- And finally, it would be even better to speak about the experience of the risen, living, and active Christ.

Chapter 4

Christ, the Supreme Mystic

Christian mystics discover their original source in the supreme mystic, Jesus of Nazareth, whose mystical experience did not consist in a succession of more or less extraordinary experiences. His was rather a continual process of self-identity, of discovering his mission in the context of his own family, society, culture, and religion. That is how Jesus grew, slowly but surely, in the Mystery of God. That, however, does not take away from the fact that Jesus' self-awareness, as Son of the Father sent into the world, reached a high point on the day of his baptism, as well as on Mount Tabor, in the Garden of Gethsemane, and on Calvary. And he arrived at the mystical height and depth of the Mystery in the experience of his resurrection.

The sermons at the Last Supper[1] show how Saint John understands Jesus' awareness of his special relationship with God the Father, a relationship that is both differentiated and undifferentiated: they are one and they are not one. This experience of unity in diversity and diversity in unity is only possible through love, because love simultaneously unites and differentiates. Jesus' mystical experience is both eminently trinitarian and, at the same time, messianic, so that his experience is one of intimacy with the trinitarian God and also of the saving will of the God of Love.

But Jesus is not just a model for all Christians of what mystical life is. He is also *the image of the invisible God,*[2] *the reflection of God's*

[1] Especially in Jn 17.
[2] Col 1:15. See also 2:9.

40

glory, and *the exact imprint of God's very being*,[3] which is why he is the only way to arrive at the Father's house[4] and the one in whom we contemplate the face of God.[5] Thus, Christ in his humanity, and in the mysteries of his death and resurrection, is the foundation of Christian mysticism. Saint John invites us to strive after union with Christ and to *abide in him*,[6] because eternal life is essentially *knowing the Father and the one whom he has sent*.[7]

Let us look for a moment at Jesus' own experience in the different stages of his public life: during his baptism, in his life as an itinerant preacher, in the Garden of Olives, and on Calvary, with a brief reference also to his resurrection and his life in glory, for there is nothing more Christian than Christ's own experience of the Mystery.

Baptism

What interests us here is to go beyond the gospel narratives in order to understand what happened historically. Looking closely at the facts, we can say first of all that Jesus' baptism is a historical event that occasioned something of a scandal. Is Jesus less important than John the Baptist?[8] Jesus was one of many persons approaching John. Then, at a signal or word from the Baptizer, he is submerged in the waters of the Jordan, as the evangelists tell us,[9] "when all the people were baptized, and when Jesus also had been baptized."[10]

All the evangelists witness to the descent of the Spirit, although the details vary according to the particular approach of each gospel. The meaning of the event consists in its being the inauguration of the prophetic ministry of Jesus. God's Spirit rests

[3] Heb 1:3.
[4] Jn 14:2; Eph 2:18.
[5] 2 Cor 4:6.
[6] Jn 6:56; 15:4-16.
[7] Jn 17:3.
[8] Mt 3:14-15.
[9] Mk 1:9.
[10] Lk 3:21. See Jn 1:26: "Among you stands one whom you do not know."

upon him to show that he is God's final and definitive eschatological messenger.[11] In the same way, all the accounts agree that
there was a solemn, divine proclamation from heaven, although
once again they differ when it comes to the details. The proclamation interprets the descent of the Spirit as the fulfillment of Isaiah
42:1: "Here is my servant, whom I uphold, my chosen, in whom
my soul delights; I have put my Spirit upon him; he will bring
forth justice to the nations."

- Mark 1:11 and Matthew 3:17: "You are [This is] my Son, the
  Beloved; with you I am well pleased."

- Luke 3:22: "You are my Son, the Beloved; with you I am well
  pleased."

- John 1:34: "I myself have seen and have testified that this is
  the Son of God."

According to the Synoptic Gospels, what happened at Christ's
baptism can be understood as something that he himself experienced: "Just as he was coming up out of the water, he saw . . .";
"When Jesus also had been baptized and was praying, the heaven
was opened."[12] This is in contrast to John's gospel, which says
that it was the Baptizer who saw.[13] But what does such an experience mean for Jesus? The experience of his baptism had a double
significance for him: it showed him that he was Son in relation
to God the Father and that he had power coming from the Spirit.
That is how he had a special understanding of his identity and
of his mission, an understanding that he immediately put into
practice.

It is possible that the idea of being Servant of the Lord, as
prophesied in Isaiah 42, was already in the mind of Jesus; but on
the day of his baptism, the text came to signify something very
special in relation to his mission:

---

[11] Mt 5:17.
[12] Mk 1:10; Lk 3:21.
[13] Jn 1:33-34.

> He will not cry or lift up his voice, or make it heard in the street;
> a bruised reed he will not break, and a dimly burning wick he
> will not quench. . . . I am the Lord, I have called you in righ-
> teousness, I have taken you by the hand and kept you; I have
> given you as a covenant to the people, a light to the nations, to
> open the eyes that are blind, to bring out the prisoners from
> the dungeon, from the prison those who sit in darkness.[14]

Jesus seems to have given great importance to the moment of
his baptism, since in one of his controversies with the authorities
he referred to his baptismal experience as the source of his authority, as if to say: "My authority is based on what happened
when I was baptized by John in the Jordan."[15]

On the day of his baptism, Jesus received an extremely important revelation both about himself and about God. God reveals
himself to Jesus as a father reveals himself to his son—that is,
fully, as his *Abba*. It is not strange, therefore, that some years later
Jesus says: "All things have been handed over to me by my
Father; and no one knows the Son except the Father, and no one
knows the Father except the Son and anyone to whom the Son
chooses to reveal him."[16]

The linguistic and stylistic features of this last text from Matthew's gospel point to a Semitic way of speaking and thinking
rather than to either a Greek or a Johannine influence. For in-
stance, "have been handed over to me" (*paredóthê*, in the aorist
tense) indicates a single past event, which must be his baptism!
John 5:19-20,[17] on the contrary, is in the present tense.

The Father revealed the Mystery to Jesus, the Mystery of his
being the Son of God the Father, and the Mystery of his will to

---

[14] Is 42:2-3, 6-7.

[15] See Mk 11:29-30: "I will tell you by what authority I do these things. Did
the baptism of John come from heaven, or was it of human origin?"

[16] Mt 11:27.

[17] "The Son can do nothing on his own, but only what he sees the Father
doing; for whatever the Father does, the Son does likewise. The Father loves
the Son and shows him all that he himself is doing."

save the world through Jesus' messianic labor. Jesus is to communicate all this to others, which is precisely what he does:

- The mystery of the kingdom is revealed to the disciples.[18]

- Jesus reveals these things to infants.[19]

- The disciples see and hear what the former prophets and righteous people did not know.[20]

- Jesus comes to fulfill revelation.[21]

Thus, through his baptismal experience, Jesus discovers his identity as Son, the continual presence of the Father in his life, the power of the Spirit who dwells in him, and his mission to be achieved through the proclamation of his kingdom and through suffering. In other words, from within his deepest identity he discovers a mystery to be revealed and a mission to be accomplished by himself.

Transfiguration and Joy

Now we can look more closely at two key moments in the life of Jesus as he made his way through Galilee. Although it is difficult to appreciate Jesus' inner experience underlying the written accounts, we will try to do so without doing violence to either the texts or the historical reality. We should take note of the fact that these two events are described in at least two, if not three, of the Synoptic Gospels, which points to their historical veracity.

The three evangelists tell us about the transfiguration on the mountain after Jesus had announced his passion and resurrection for the first time and had instructed his disciples to follow him in the way of self-denial and the cross. This intuition concerning his destiny and the experience of transfiguration are thus inti-

---

[18] Mk 4:11.
[19] Mt 11:25.
[20] Mt 13:16-17.
[21] See Mt 5:17.

mately connected in Jesus' life. The transfiguration on the mountain seems to be an experience of new strength to face the prospect of a future replete with suffering.

According to Mark's account, which is chronologically the oldest of the three, Jesus says that the one who loses his life for him and for the Gospel will find it. He then prophesies: "Truly I tell you, there are some standing here who will not taste death until they see that the kingdom of God has come with power."[22] Who are these "some who will not taste death" until they first experience the power of God's kingdom? It is an obvious reference to the three disciples who climbed up the mountain with him; but what I want to stress is that Jesus himself is the first one to experience the power of the kingdom in his own flesh.

Mark writes: "He was transfigured before them, and his clothes became dazzling white, such as no one on earth could bleach them. And there appeared to them Elijah with Moses, who were talking with Jesus."[23] Luke goes into more detail: Jesus "went up on the mountain to pray. And while he was praying, the appearance of his face changed, and his clothes became dazzling white. Suddenly they saw two men, Moses and Elijah, talking to him. They appeared in glory and were speaking of his departure [*éxodon*], which he was about to accomplish at Jerusalem."[24]

The kingdom of God is the proclamation of victory over death with joyful, overflowing life for all, especially for someone like Jesus, who is on his way to death on a cross. The transfiguration is an anticipation of the resurrection, a foretaste preparing Jesus for total submersion in the horror of his passion, which will lead him to Life. At the end of the narrative, they all are submerged in the divine mystery symbolized by "a cloud [that] overshadowed them, and from the cloud there came a voice, 'This is my Son, the Beloved; listen to him!'"[25] Jesus feels newly strengthened and reaffirmed in the mission that was revealed to him at his

[22] Mk 9:1.
[23] Mk 9:2-4.
[24] Lk 9:28-31.
[25] Mk 9:7.

baptism.[26] God himself works and speaks through him, which is why he must be listened to.

Now let us look at his experience of ecstatic joy, beginning with its place in Jesus' life. He gradually realizes that the day of his departure, his exodus, is approaching: "When the days drew near for him to be taken up, he set his face to go to Jerusalem."[27] After describing to his disciples the demands of their apostolic vocation, Jesus instructs them and sends seventy-two of them on a mission, which turns out to be highly successful. The disciples return and tell him how they could experience the *power* that Jesus gave them to make the demons submit to them, a sign that the kingdom of God has arrived.[28] At that very moment of their conversation, "Jesus rejoiced in the Holy Spirit and said, 'I thank you, Father, Lord of heaven and earth, because you have hidden these things from the wise and the intelligent and have revealed them to infants; yes, Father, for such was your gracious will. All things have been handed over to me by my Father; and no one knows who the Son is except the Father, or who the Father is except the Son and anyone to whom the Son chooses to reveal him.'"[29]

It is important to look well at what was happening to Jesus when he "rejoiced [*êgalliásato*] in the Holy Spirit." It was an experience that can be understood as an "ecstasy of joy." But what was the cause of his rejoicing? There seems to have been a triple cause. In the first place, he rejoiced at seeing that God's kingdom overcomes the kingdom of the evil one. Then, too, he rejoiced at the experience of the Father's mercy revealed to infants and hidden from the great and the wise. This makes us remember how likewise Mary's "spirit rejoices [*êgallíasen*] in God"[30] when she realizes that she has been looked upon by God because of her lowliness and that, in the same way, the proud have been scat-

---

[26] See Mk 1:11.
[27] Lk 9:51.
[28] See Lk 9:57–10:20.
[29] Lk 10:21-22.
[30] Lk 1:47.

tered, the powerful brought down, and the rich and prosperous sent away empty.[31] Finally, Jesus rejoices in his deep, intimate knowledge of the Father and his awareness that the Father has handed everything over to him, especially the revelation of the Father's mystery to the smallest children. The disciples, who are witnesses of all this, are, for that reason, more "blessed" than many prophets and kings.[32]

Gethsemane

Underlying the account given by the evangelists, it is easy to discern here the nucleus of what Jesus' experience in the Garden of Gethsemane was—namely, his relationship with his disciples and with God his Father. Jesus is alone, and the disciples have reached the nadir of their lack of understanding[33] and are at a distance from their Master. But is Jesus really alone, or is he with his Father?

Jesus' relationship with his Father is experienced by him through a few symbols full of pathos and the prayerful gift of self in spite of the silence. The chalice is the visible manifestation of the invisible will of the Father, equivalent to the "hour." It is God's mysterious plan for humanity, what is divinely and irrevocably decided, which therefore must be set into motion. It is, briefly stated, the handing over of Jesus into the hands of sinners, the saving death of the Servant and of the Just One, and his being lifted up on high so as to draw all to himself that is the glorification of Jesus and the Father.

Jesus prays that, if possible, the chalice pass him by without his drinking it, but in the end he accepts it from the depths of his heart: "Not what I want, but what you want. Am I not to drink the cup that the Father has given me?"[34] The inspired author of the Letter to the Hebrews tells us that Jesus hands himself over

---

[31] Lk 1:51-53.
[32] Lk 10:23-24.
[33] Mk 4:13.
[34] Mk 14:36; Jn 18:11.

to "the one who was able to save him from death,"[35] and he does so *with prayers*—insistent entreaties based on his own poverty and need—*and supplications*, which stresses even more strongly the radical urgency of his prayers, and *with loud cries and tears*, like those of the righteous hero of Psalm 21(22):3-25, so that he would be saved from death.

Faced with the chalice, Jesus "threw himself on the ground,"[36] which Matthew and Luke show to be a sign of deep acceptance. Mark's version is more dramatic and even gives the impression that Jesus was humanly torn apart. In other words, the threatening presence of the chalice is a cause of frightful terror. Jesus' experience, so fraught with pathos, as presented so forcefully by the evangelists, shows us

- *his sadness*,[37] the opposite of joy, since it is the lack of what is good—was it due to the Father's absence?—it was not a simple sadness, however, but a mortal one, a deep grief "even to death"[38];

- *his distress*,[39] interior anguish, agitation, and unrest, similar to the result of a deep convulsion;

- *his agony*,[40] anxiety, and sweating of blood, his need for strengthening by an angel for the combat[41];

- *his trouble of soul*,[42] like what he had experienced at Mary's weeping for the death of her brother, Lazarus,[43] or like the experience of the disciples at hearing that Jesus would be betrayed by one of them, that Peter would deny him, and that Jesus would leave them.[44]

[35] Heb 5:7.
[36] Mt 26:39.
[37] Mt 26:37-38; Mk 14:34.
[38] Mk 14:34. See Ps 41(42):5, "Why are you cast down my soul, why groan within me?"
[39] Mt 26:37; Mk 14:33.
[40] See Lk 22:44: "His sweat became like great drops of blood."
[41] Lk 22:43.
[42] Jn 12:27.
[43] Jn 11:33.
[44] Jn 14:1: "Do not let your hearts be troubled."

Jesus turns his fear, discouragement, self-offering, and acceptance into prayer. His Father keeps silent, his hand remains over
the whole scene, and the chalice continues to be offered to his
beloved Son. The Father is present, yet absent. Jesus accepts the
fact, the chalice, in naked faith and divine silence. He knows that
there is only one road to follow in order to establish the kingdom
of divine communion among God's children, only one way to
have God's mysterious plan fully and effectively revealed in all
its power—namely, by offering himself up to death and surren-
dering his life into the hands of sinners.

Jesus instinctively wants to prolong his life, although his will
is to be faithful to the Father, and *he learned obedience through what
he suffered*.[45] He had identified himself with the mission he had
received. He had become man and had revealed the kingdom in
an admirable way, but the result is that he is going to die without
establishing the kingdom on earth! This chalice seems to go
against setting up the kingdom. His entire life's work seems to
be collapsing. Only one road is open to him, that of blindly giving
himself over to death.

Now it is not only his enemies who reject him; his friends do
so, too. Judas betrays him and the disciples go to sleep, then deny
knowing him, and will soon show their cowardice by fleeing
from him. But despite it all, Jesus accepts his destiny as the will
of the Father, and he drinks his cup to the dregs. In the midst of
this total abandonment he remains united to God and continues
to call out to him, "Abba, my Father."[46] In other words, he remains
faithful to his original experience of God and to its deepest mystery. He sinks into the open jaws of death and into the unfathom-
able abyss of God's mysterious plan.

Calvary

As a prologue to the silence of death, the last words of someone
still living are usually significant as a synthesis of all his past.
They usually imply both a personal experience and a final message

[45] Heb 5:8.
[46] See Mk 14:36.

for posterity. That is why the last words of Jesus on the cross before he gives up his spirit are so moving. The evangelists give different versions of these words, but these differences pertain only to emphasis since the underlying facts and message are the same:

- Mark: Were there two cries? Perhaps the second one was wordless: "Jesus cried out with a loud voice, 'Eloi, Eloi, lema sabachthani?' which means, 'My God, my God, why have you forsaken me?' . . . Then Jesus gave a loud cry and breathed his last."[47]

- Matthew: there were two cries, for the second one no words are given: "Jesus cried with a loud voice, 'Eli, Eli, lema sabachthani?' that is, 'My God, my God, why have you forsaken me?' . . . Then Jesus cried again with a loud voice and breathed his last."[48]

- Luke tells of a cry with spoken words: "Then Jesus, crying with a loud voice, said, 'Father, into your hands I commend my spirit.' Having said this, he breathed his last."[49]

- John speaks not of any cry but only of one word: "He said, 'It is finished.' Then he bowed his head and gave up his spirit."[50]

The obvious fact is the following: Jesus died *crucified* and *crying out with a loud voice*, something out of the ordinary for someone crucified and dying of asphyxiation. That is why the centurion was so amazed that when he "saw that in this way he breathed his last, he said, 'Truly this man was God's Son!' "[51]

Now, what was Jesus' cry when he breathed his last? Those who were there thought they heard Jesus cry out for Elijah (ʾ*Eliyahu,*

---

[47] Mk 15:34, 37.
[48] Mt 27:46, 50.
[49] Lk 23:46.
[50] Jn 19:30.
[51] Mk 15:39.

abbreviated to *'Eliya*). But how did they interpret *'Eliya ta'* ("Elijah, come") from *'Eloí*, as in Mark, or from *'Elí*, as in Matthew? Perhaps what Jesus said, which occasioned the confusion, was *'Elí 'atta* ("You are my God").

This loud cry "You are my God" (*'Elí 'atta*), appears in Scripture seven different times. Apart from Isaiah 44:17 and Psalm 142(143):10, the other four times are highly significant:

- Psalm 21(22):11—the concluding words of the abandoned just man's lament. Note that Psalm 21(22):19, on casting lots for the clothing, appears in the passion narratives of Mark, Matthew, and John, and verse 2, *My God, my God*, is in Matthew and John.

- Psalm 30(31):15—a prayer in time of trial, inspired by Jeremiah. Note that the words "Into your hands I commend my spirit" of Psalm 30(31):6 appear in Luke's narrative.

- Psalm 62(63):2—a prayer on *thirsting for God*. There is a reference to thirst in John's narrative,[52] as well as in Psalms 21(22):16 and 68(69):22.

- Psalm 117(118):28—this is the concluding psalm of the paschal *Hallel* (Psalms 112[113]–117[118]). Both Matthew and Mark refer to it.[53]

All the foregoing helps us to understand Jesus' experience on the cross. Jesus dies reciting Psalm 21(22) in Hebrew, whose verse 11 says, *'Elí 'atta* ("You are my God"), which for someone whose native language is Aramaic could sound like *'Eliya tá* ("Elijah, come"). By dying with the words *'Elí 'atta* ("You are my God") on his lips, Jesus shows his radical, even violent, trust in God, thus continuing the same union with his Father that he had proclaimed in Gethsemane. Despite all his pain, he dies proclaiming that God is his God, that is, his Father. Like the persecuted just man that he is, and like all who thirst for God in the desert of

[52] Jn 19:28.
[53] Mt 26:30; Mk 14:26.

abandonment, Jesus dies with the final words of the great *Hallel* on his lips, celebrating the ultimate triumph of God over the enemies of the covenant.

Jesus on the cross was in a desperate *situation*; but *he himself* was not desperate. God had not abandoned him as such, but had only abandoned him into helplessness at the hands of the enemies. Jesus never lacked faith, only its lights and its radiance.

Resurrection

Jesus had prayed in Gethsemane: "Not what I want, but what you want."[54] On Calvary he cried out in the throes of death: "You are my God." Nothing could be truer. God was his God, his Father, and therefore he is freed from death through resurrection, although passing through death. But how can we describe Jesus' experience at the moment of his resurrection? As children in the Son, let us contemplate the mystery:

- By suffering such abandonment[55] and entrusting himself into the hands of the Father,[56] Jesus embraced an adventure that could only end well, which is why he is blessed and why the blessings of his Beatitudes are true.[57] Condemned by men, he was exonerated by God, and the Creator's "Yes!" rang gloriously in his ears, silencing the accursed "No!" of creatures.[58] Having become sin for us, he experienced in his own flesh the victory over sin and death.[59]

- His mortal body was transformed into a spiritual one, *a life-giving spirit*,[60] and he saw himself created anew like a new man, a New Adam, the firstborn of those risen from the

---

[54] Mk 14:36.
[55] See Mt 15:44.
[56] See Lk 23:46.
[57] See Lk 6:20-23 and Mt 5:1-12.
[58] See Acts 2:22-28.
[59] See Rom 8:3 and 2 Cor 5:21.
[60] 1 Cor 15:44-45.

dead.[61] He sprang to life again in his divine sonship[62] and saw that it is he who gives the Spirit.[63] He thus was given the name that is above all names[64] and experienced the perfection of his incarnation because the whole fullness of deity began to dwell bodily in him.[65]

- He even multiplied his saving presence, since he is the fullness of him who fills all in all[66] and thus can become identified with the persecuted and the little ones[67] and can hide himself in the eucharistic mystery under the appearance of bread and wine.[68]

There is no doubt that the resurrection is for Jesus a deeply theological experience of God and of his transforming, divine action. This experience is the key for understanding the silence of the evangelists concerning the manner of the resurrection. Encountering the Ineffable One is itself an ineffable reality. It also helps us understand the different experiences of the disciples when they meet their Risen Master, since the accounts of these apparitions are human attempts to communicate the incommunicable.

The Bridegroom

Salvation history, like the covenant with its mediators and prophets, converges on Jesus Christ. In him, humanity and God himself are united in a nuptial embrace. Messianic times, celebrating the marriage between God and his people, begin with the arrival of Jesus, the Bridegroom, which is precisely the

[61] Rom 5:7; 1 Cor 15:20-23.
[62] See Rom 1:3-4.
[63] See Jn 20:22.
[64] Phil 2:9.
[65] Col 2:9.
[66] Eph 1:23.
[67] See Acts 9:5 and Mt 25:31-46.
[68] See Mt 26:26-27 and parallels.

testimony of John the Baptizer, precursor and "friend of the bridegroom."[69]

It is not surprising that Jesus, too, experienced it this way. It explains why he presented his message about the kingdom of God in the form of a wedding feast.[70] We can also recall his words at the Passover supper during his final farewells: "I tell you, I will never again drink of this fruit of the vine until that day when I drink it new with you in my Father's kingdom."[71]

In the book of Revelation we find a fuller development than what is outlined in Paul's letter to the Ephesians[72] concerning the nuptial relationship between Christ and his Church. In the spousal relationship we can find the eschatological experience of the Risen Christ in his relationship with us. The Risen Jesus experiences himself as the Bridegroom of the Church and the Spouse of each and every Christian. That is how he lives the mystery of the divine plan of salvation.

Five texts concerning this spousal identity of Christ merit our attention.

Christ the Bridegroom is present among us with solicitous spousal love as the one who "nourishes and tenderly cares for" us.[73] So it is not strange that he has a divine "zeal" for our salvation and does everything possible to present us to himself without spot or wrinkle, but holy and without blemish before him in love. That explains the strong words addressed to the Churches of Ephesus and Laodicea: "I have this against you, that you have abandoned the love you had at first. Remember then from what you have fallen; repent, and do the works you did at first"[74]; and "I know your works; you are neither cold nor hot. I wish that you were either cold or hot. So, because you are lukewarm, and neither cold nor hot, I am about to spit you out of my mouth."[75]

[69] Jn 3:29.
[70] In Mt 22:1-14.
[71] Mt 26:29.
[72] See Eph 5:21-23.
[73] Eph 5:29.
[74] Rev 2:4-5.
[75] Rev 3:15-16.

Here, the Bridegroom is lamenting and complaining about the little love shown him by his bride, just as the Lord did when he complained about the unfaithfulness of his people—his wife—calling her back to the love of her youth, as in the days of her desert experience.[76]

But the final word of the Bridegroom is not a threat filled with the zeal of passionate love. Rather, he promises and explains a deeper communion in the messianic banquet, saying: "I reprove and discipline those whom I love. Be earnest, therefore, and repent. Listen! I am standing at the door, knocking; if you hear my voice and open the door, I will come in to you and eat with you, and you with me."[77] These words of the Risen Bridegroom echo those of the Song of Songs: "Open to me, my sister, my love, my dove, my perfect one."[78]

Christ the Bridegroom is aflame with the desire to celebrate forever his eternal wedding feast with the Church, his bride. That is why, throughout the long history of our journey, he helps us "to be clothed with fine linen, bright and pure," for that is the only way we will be able to share in the wedding feast of the Lamb and the Bride.[79] We will be all together at that banquet, united among ourselves and with him.[80] Christ the Bridegroom always hears the groans of love from his bride, who is full of the Spirit: "Come, Lord Jesus!" And his reply is always there: "Surely I am coming soon."[81]

Jesus' mystical experience is the model and the foundation of all Christian mystical experience. In Jesus Christ, the experience of God and the Mystery of God are historically and harmoniously identified at their highest level because *Jesus is the Mystery of God*.[82] Our mystical experience is wholly the experience of his

[76] See Hos 3:16-22.
[77] Rev 3:19-20.
[78] Song 5:2.
[79] Rev 19:5-9.
[80] See Rev 21:9-14.
[81] Rev 22:20.
[82] Rom 16:25-27 and Col 1:26.

Mystery: *to live in Christ, to die and rise again with him.*[83] This experience, which will reach its climax in the next world, has already begun here and now, with the Spirit and the bride crying, "Come!" and the Bridegroom answering, "Surely I am coming soon."[84]

[83] See Gal 2:20 and Phil 3:10.
[84] Rev 22:17, 20.

Chapter 5

Our Mystical Experience

The richer the objective reality revealed to us, the deeper will be its transforming experience in the life of each particular person. It is dangerous to forget that moral behavior needs dogma and that spirituality, which is *living* faith, needs theology, that is, *understanding* of the faith. After all, isn't mysticism the flowering of revealed truth, which in its turn is the root of mysticism?

A healthy balance reigned throughout the entire twelfth century—often called the "Cistercian century"—between the objective and subjective aspects of Christian mysticism. Revelation was looked upon not as a series of truths external to the human person but as life-transforming realities that fulfill the person because it satisfies the deepest desires of the human heart. Personal experience was always governed by the objectivity of what had been revealed. Thus, mysticism is the reality of grace accompanying the whole life of the believer, transforming him or her from dawn into midday and from an individual burning coal into an all-consuming fire.

Cîteaux knew how to put the accent on life or, more exactly, on Christian faith as a unified and lived experience in which all dimensions of the person are taken up and hierarchically integrated. The relation of each human being with God embraces all our humanity, so that body, psyche, and spirit journey together toward the divine Being, who has revealed himself by touching us in the Person of Jesus Christ.

Experience is a foundational element in the teaching of the early Cistercians, simply because all their spirituality is based on love. So it is not strange that they invite us to share their experience and ardently want us to do so:

> Let your voice sound in my ears, good Jesus, so that my heart may learn how to love you, my mind how to love you, the inmost being of my soul how to love you. Let the inmost core of my heart embrace you, my one and only true good, my dear and delightful joy. . . . I pray you, Lord, let but a drop of your surpassing sweetness fall upon my soul, that by it the bread of her bitterness may become sweet. In experiencing a drop of this may she have a foretaste of what to desire, what to long for, what to sigh for here on her pilgrimage. In her hunger let her have a foretaste, in her thirst let her drink. For those who eat you will still hunger and those who drink you will still thirst.[1]

In the teaching of Bernard of Clairvaux and Aelred of Rievaulx, the most frequent use of the word "experience"—and the most common occurrence of the spiritual reality—is found in their descriptions of spiritual search and spiritual progress. In other words, it is a question of the experience of love at the different stages and steps of one's journey toward God. The clearest and strongest manifestation of this experience of love consists in one's free consent to the divine will: "Seek the Word that you may assent to him [*cui consentias*]; it is he who gives you the grace of assenting."[2]

For our authors, the ascetical experience and the mystical experience are two realities joined in the single supernatural journey toward God. When they speak of God, they are not forgetting the human subject. They know that before ascending to the heaven of the spirit, one has to descend to the dark caves of the human soul. They even tell us that whoever descends in this manner is really going up. Obviously, our Fathers were acquainted with mystical experience properly so-called, although they do not always emphasize its more or less extraordinary characteristics, and they refer to it with a wide variety of words

---

[1] Aelred of Rievaulx, *Mirror of Charity* 1.1.2.
[2] Bernard, *Song* 85.1.

and symbols: *rest, Sabbath, ecstasy, visits, rapture, kisses, embrace, union, elevation, marriage, unity of spirit, deification.*

This type of experience can refer both to the Mystery of God's intimate triune life and to the Mystery of his saving will, both of which come to us through the Risen Son and in his Spirit. In our context as monks and nuns marked by the Cistercian tradition, the most common experiences of the Lord's Mystery often have to do with

- the liberating goodness and friendship of God (*dulcedo et suavitas*);

- compunction of heart (*compunctio*);

- the desert and its attractive, transforming darkness (*desertum*);

- desire for what is infinite and absolute (*desiderium*);

- a spousal covenant with the Beloved (*sponsalia*);

- communion of wills (*unitas spiritus*);

- alternating succession of spiritual phenomena (*alternatio*).

It may be helpful to say something about each one of these experiences, even though we know that some of them overlap. We will refer to the witness of biblical and patristic tradition to show their contemporary relevance and importance. Needless to say, the intensity, clarity, and fruits of these experiences vary according to the circumstances and because of a thousand other factors that often cannot be analyzed. In all cases, however, it is a question of differing ways for entering into the Mystery of the Lord.

Sweetness and Kindness (*Dulcedo et Suavitas*)

Sacred Scripture often talks about the goodness, sweetness, and kindness of God, which clearly implies that the inspired authors have experienced him with these qualities. Let us look at a few examples of this:

The Lord is good [*dulcis*] and upright.
He shows the path to those who stray.[3]

How great is the goodness [*multitudo dulcedinis*], Lord,
that you keep for those who fear you,
that you show to those who trust you.[4]

Taste and see that the Lord is good [*suavis*].
He is happy who seeks refuge in him.[5]

Rid yourselves, therefore, of all malice, and all guile, insincerity, envy, and all slander. Like newborn infants, long for the pure, spiritual milk, so that by it you may grow into salvation—if indeed you have tasted that the Lord is good [*si tamen gustastis quoniam dulcis est Dominus*].[6]

The essence of these four quotations is the invitation of Psalm 33(34): "Taste and see that the Lord is good," which finds its echo in the text from 1 Peter. We should note that these texts also refer to tasting as a spiritual sense. The sense of taste refers simultaneously to the act itself of tasting something and also to what it tastes like, its flavor. It is a question of an experience in which the distance between the person tasting and the object tasted is reduced to a minimum. It is thus an experience that is hard to objectify and is therefore almost incommunicable. So it is not surprising that the experience of taste often refers to the love of God in some of his attributes.

Our monastic patriarch, Saint Benedict, says in his Rule that the call to monastic life is often lived as an experience of divine goodness: "What, dear brothers, is more delightful [*dulcius*] than this voice of the Lord calling to us?"[7] And further on he encourages us with this statement based on his own experience: "As we progress in this way of life and in faith, we shall run on the path

---

[3] Ps 24(25):8.
[4] Ps 30(31):20.
[5] Ps 33(34):9.
[6] 1 Pet 2:1-3.
[7] RB Prol. 19.

of God's commandments, our hearts overflowing with the inexpressible delight [*dulcedine*] of love."[8]

Let us look more closely at this clear reference to Benedict's personal experience. The sentence, which is original to Benedict himself, seems to be inspired by three biblical texts:

> I will run the way of your commands;
> you give freedom to my heart.[9]

> You love him [Jesus]; and even though you do not see him now, you believe in him and rejoice with an indescribable and glorious joy.[10]

> My yoke is easy, and my burden is light.[11]

In the light of these biblical sources, the statement of our patriarch becomes clearer. It is God himself who fills the monk's heart with his presence and so makes it overflow with the delight of an inexpressible sweetness. The inexpressible quality of the experience points to its properly mystical nature, although it is not just any experience that can do this but only one that falls within the context of biblical revelation, which Benedict refers to as "God's commandments." The God who is present is a God who acts, which is why monks can "praise the Lord working in them."[12]

But how can the experience of the "inexpressible delight of love" be compatible with the other experience by which "we shall through patience share in the sufferings of Christ"?[13] Actually, there is no contradiction between the two experiences; in fact, authentic monastic life implies an alternation between joy and sorrow, since it is precisely the delightful sweetness that lets someone suffer with Christ and patience in trial that obtains the ineffable consolation. In any case, the important point is that this

---

[8] RB Prol. 49.
[9] Ps 118(119):32.
[10] 1 Pet 1:8.
[11] Mt 11:30.
[12] RB Prol. 30.
[13] RB Prol. 50.

experience of death and new life is part of the Paschal Mystery, which explains why it is not surprising that it produces good fruit for the whole body of the Church.[14]

To understand this experience better, it helps to see it in the context of Saint Bernard's teaching on the experiences of divine love. In his book *On Loving God*, Bernard offers a step-by-step guide to love.[15] The five successive experiences of love are as follows:

1. Love of self for one's own sake (*propter seipsum*): natural love

2. Love of neighbor (*consortem naturae*): social love
   - for the neighbor's sake as well as for one's own benefit (*amor justus*)
   - for God's sake (*amor purus*)

3. Love of God for one's own benefit (*propter se*): prudent love

4. Love of God for God's sake (*propter Ipsum*): gratuitous love

5. Love of self for the sake of God (*seipsum propter Deum*): transforming love

Here we are interested in a particular aspect of Bernard's map of the journey: the experience of the "passage" from prudent love (which is both necessary and self-interested) to gratuitous love. Bernard gives two explanations, which differ but complement each other, one on the basis of *liberation*, the other on the basis of *familiarity* or *friendship*. Both approaches lead to tasting the goodness of the Lord. Sweetness (*dulcedo*) and kindness or gentleness (*suavitas*) are two divine attributes that express God's goodness metaphorically by underlining his pleasing presence, attractiveness, and charm:

> If man's tribulations grow in frequency and as a result he frequently turns to God and is frequently freed by God, must man not in the end—even though he had a heart of stone in a breast of iron—come to realize that it is God's grace which frees him,

---

[14] See Col 1:24.

[15] See Bernard, *On Loving God* 23–33, 39–40.

and come to love God not for his own advantage but for the sake of God? Man's frequent needs oblige him to invoke God more often and approach him more frequently. This intimacy moves man to taste and discover how sweet the Lord is. Tasting God's sweetness entices us more to pure love than does the urgency of our own needs.[16]

When forced by his own needs, man begins to honor God and care for him by thinking of him, reading about him, praying to him, and obeying him. God reveals himself gradually in this kind of familiarity and consequently becomes lovable. When man tastes how sweet God is, he passes to the third degree of love in which man loves God not now because of himself but because of God. No doubt man remains a long time in this degree.[17]

Any monk or nun who has patiently persevered in the monastic way of life can bear witness to the *sweetness of love* and the painful *patience* that are always simultaneously present in their lives. For my part, I want to emphasize, above all, the experiences of *freedom* and of *familiarity* with God as a friend, which flow from the tribulations of *lectio divina* and obedience. Both of them convert the human heart so that it can taste the delightful goodness of God as liberator and friend. Such an experience makes concrete and interiorizes these realities of faith, which we were familiar with before in only an abstract or impersonal way. This not infrequently marks the beginning of a new stage in one's spiritual journey, a certain transformation of the heart that causes someone who was previously seeking God to adhere to him not for the sake of tasting his goodness but because God is good in himself. God grants us the experience of what Baldwin of Ford wrote about in his treatise on the *Sacrament of the Altar*:

Jesus is sweet and his name is sweet. His "name and renown are the soul's desire."[18] He is sweet when he receives our desires, calms our grief, puts an end to our sighs, and dries our

---

[16] Bernard, *On Loving God*, 26. See also *Song* 36.6.
[17] Bernard, *On Loving God* 39.
[18] Is 26:8.

tears. . . . He is sweet in prayer, sweet in conversations, sweet in *lectio*, sweet in contemplation, sweet both in compunction and in joy of heart, sweet in the mouth, sweet in the heart, and sweet when we love him. He is the love of sweetness and the sweetness of love. His unspeakable gentleness is first among his gifts and greatest among all delights. Those who taste him will still hunger for more, and those who hunger for him will be filled; then, once filled, they will praise him forever and will recall his abundant goodness.[19]

Compunction (*Compunctio*)

We are well acquainted with the results of Peter's preaching on the day of Pentecost: "When they heard this, they were cut to the heart and said to Peter and to the other apostles, 'Brothers, what should we do?' "[20] This text is the necessary point of reference for the ongoing foundational experience of compunction in Christian and monastic spirituality. It is basically an experience of being "punctured" in order to be made aware of one's real condition before God, whether this reality be that of an ungrateful offender or that of a mercifully pardoned and much-loved sinner. Saint Gregory the Great speaks about compunction in terms of a homesick desire for heaven and its kingdom.

Monastic witnesses overflow with testimonies of compunction. It is one of the most common experiences, except in the lives of mediocre monks since, according to Bernard of Clairvaux, "their compunction is not constant, but intermittent, . . . fleeting and infrequent."[21] Few of us, of course, can say what we hear about Abba Arsenius: "It was said of him that he had a hollow in his chest channeled out by the tears which fell from his eyes all his life while he sat at his manual work."[22]

For Saint Benedict, compunction is a good work at which "to toil faithfully . . . [within] the enclosure of the monastery and

[19] Baldwin of Ford, *Sacrament of the Altar*, conclusion.
[20] Acts 2:37.
[21] Bernard, *Sermons on the Lord's Ascension* 3.7 and 6.7.
[22] *The Sayings of the Desert Fathers: The Alphabetical Collection*, trans. B. Ward; Arsenius, n. 41.

stability in the community."[23] Even more, it is a key instrument for a pure life during Lent and for living the rest of our life, which "we can do in a fitting manner by refusing to indulge evil habits and by devoting ourselves to prayer with tears, to reading, to compunction of heart and self-denial."[24]

The Benedictine monk, saying in his heart that he is not worthy to look up to heaven,[25] establishes a deep communion with the compunction of the Heart of Jesus himself—that is, with his deepest, most ardent longing for the final establishment of the kingdom of heaven. This is so because one of the fruits of compunction is to "look forward to holy Easter with joy and spiritual longing."[26]

The impression could be given that this emphasis on compunction would convert monks and nuns into sad melancholics, but exactly the opposite is the case. Compunction is not the equivalent of being sad, and Benedict insists *that no one should be disquieted or distressed in the house of God.*[27] Aelred of Rievaulx, in the twelfth century, gives us a full doctrine of compunction strongly marked by his pedagogical style. It is worth noting that Aelred speaks indistinctly of *compunction* and spiritual *visitation*, distinguishing three types of such experiences.[28]

The first experience of a visitation of compunction is the work of divine *mercy* seeking the lost sheep and raising up those who have fallen. It is an experience of *fear* mixed with moments of *consolation*, given both to the reprobate for judgment and to the elect for advancement. Its purpose is to *wake people up* by showing them what is wrong in their lives so that they will return to God. The experience is fittingly symbolized by the sign of a *goad* correcting someone who is swerving out of line.

The second experience of a visitation of compunction is the work of God's *loving-kindness* reforming the one who has been

---

[23] RB 4.78.
[24] RB 49.4.
[25] See RB 7.65.
[26] RB 49.7.
[27] RB 31.19 and in six other places.
[28] See Aelred, *Mirror of Charity*, 2.4.7–8.20; 2.11.26–27; 2.12.29; 2.17.50–52.

found by divine mercy and strengthening him or her for the spiritual warfare. As opposed to the first type of experience, it is now a question of experiencing *consolation* along with a touch of *fear*. This affects two types of persons: those who will be tempted, so that they do not fall, and those who are being tempted, so that they bear the temptation more easily. Its purpose is, on the one hand, to *refresh* those in trouble by helping them in their weakness and, on the other hand, to *mortify* their self-will so that they grow in faith. What better sign could there be for this than a *staff* supporting someone weak?

The third visitation of compunction differs from the other two in that there is no negative element in it. It is the work of divine justice rewarding those who are perfect with a *charity* that casts out fear, crowning in this way those who have overcome temptation. Its purpose is to reward with total happiness those who long and sigh, thus confirming them in faith. Compunction is a *couch* receiving someone at rest in this life, in anticipation of the full rest that is to come in the next. Perhaps it would be better not to speak of being "punctured" by love, but rather to speak of being "pierced through" by its arrow.

The experience of compunction is basically an experience of spiritual awakening. It provides the motivation for conversion to God, with the necessary rejection of sin and of whatever is less than the Creator. The alternation of different experiences of compunction purifies the heart's self-centeredness and gradually configures it to the image and likeness of Christ the Lord. They can be easily interpreted as manifestations of the "good zeal" of Christ the Bridegroom. He corrects and encourages us by means of his Word, which we confront in *lectio divina.* His Word acts like a mirror of what the person is and what he or she can become through divine grace. Christ, the Spouse of every Christian, is purifying those he loves so as to prepare them for deep fellowship with him in a single spirit.

The difference between being stricken by compunction, or remorse, and having a guilt complex is obvious to any moderately discreet observer. Compunction is open to the Mystery of the Other, to reality, while a gloomy feeling of guilt is closed in on itself.

The Desert (*Desertum*)

Few persons pass any length of time in a monastery without experiencing that their growth into the Mystery involves an ever-deeper process of purifying simplification. It is precisely at the moment of growth that we feel that the contrary is taking place. Growth is lived as diminishment, nearness seems more like absence, the language of silence appears to be a conversation between deaf-mutes, and prayer in particular is felt as time lost in futility. Bernard of Clairvaux, who was above all a man of experience, talks about this:

> Whenever I begin to speak of prayer, it seems to me that I can hear the thoughts of your human hearts asking the questions which I have often been put by others, and have sometimes felt stirring in my own mind. "How is it that, although we pray almost without intermission, none of us appears hardly ever to derive any fruit from his prayer? We seem to be just the same after we have prayed as we were before. No one has answered us a word, no one seemingly has given us anything for our trouble; it looks as if we have been laboring in vain." But what does the Lord say in the Gospel? "Do not judge by appearances, but judge with right judgment."[29] Now what judgment is right if not the judgment of faith? For it is written, "The one who is righteous will live by faith."[30] Put your trust, therefore, in the judgment of faith and not in your own perception of the experience [*experimentum*], because faith is infallible, whereas your perception is liable to err. But where shall we find the truth of faith if not in the promises given by the Son of God himself, who has said, "Whatever you ask for in prayer with faith, you will receive"?[31] My brothers, none of you ought to look upon his own prayer as of little value, for I assure you, he to whom it is addressed does not regard it in that way. Before the prayer has time to leave our lips, he orders it to be registered in his own book. And when we pray we can always hope with confidence for one or other of two things: either that he

[29] Jn 7:24.
[30] Rom 1:17.
[31] Mt 21:22.

will give us what we ask or that we shall receive something else instead which he knows will be more profitable for us. "For we do not know how to pray as we ought,"[32] but he has compassion on our ignorance, and while graciously receiving our prayer, refuses to give us what would not be good for us, or defers to grant what will be more profitable bestowed later on. Our prayer, however, does not remain unfruitful.[33]

We should note here that Saint Bernard uses not the Latin word *experientia* but rather *experimentum*, that is, the result of the experience itself. Instead of saying, "Do not trust what you experience," he is actually saying, "Do not trust your interpretation made after the experience." Prayer is never fruitless. If our interpretation of an experience in prayer leads us to different conclusions, we should say that our interpretation is mistaken and should be brought in line with what faith teaches. Lack of trust in our prayer shows a great lack of faith!

This process is almost always disconcerting and leads to a spiritual crisis. What is really happening is that our superficiality is fighting against the need to live on a deeper level, and our complexity goes against any greater simplicity. We are floating corks and dry raisins: it is not easy to sink us or squash us, and when the Lord does so, it hurts.

What is most disconcerting, however, is that one's penetration into the Lord's Mystery is usually experienced as dryness, as an arid desert. In one's concrete daily life, this means a great difficulty in freely using our interior faculties—understanding, will power, memory, imagination, affectivity—during the special times dedicated to prayer. And all of it seems to have very little to do with contemplation and mysticism, at least with our preconceived ideas about them.

This obscure, yet transforming, desert experience is often sharpened during the time of thanksgiving after eucharistic Communion. This is very understandable, since the Eucharist is the

[32] Rom 8:26.
[33] Bernard, *Sermons for Lent* 5.5.

Mystery of faith that transforms the person who shares in it. There is no more mystical moment in the monastic day than the one immediately following the reception of eucharistic Communion. Appearances to the contrary notwithstanding, this Communion is an intimate union with the Risen Christ and his own Spirit. Monastic tradition and the Fathers of the Church have always associated eucharistic Communion with the presence promised by Jesus during his discourse at the Last Supper: "Those who love me will be loved by my Father, and I will love them and reveal myself to them. . . . Those who love me will keep my word, and my Father will love them, and we will come to them and make our home with them."[34]

In this theocentric desert that lets us enter into the Mystery, the impossibility of using our faculties is accompanied by other characteristic experiences, such as the absence of sensible pleasure in the things of God, as well as in those of the world; the painful yet faithful remembrance of God, combined with both a feeling of spiritual failure and a sincere desire for growth; and some type of deep, hidden peace in God, with the desire to quietly rest in him. There is no sensible consolation in this desert, but only fidelity: the Lord's toward us and ours toward the Lord.

This relative inability to use our faculties during the time of prayer can last not only for some months but for years. What precisely is happening here? To put it simply: a greater infusion of faith, hope, and love, purifying our faith from the outer embellishments of specifically distinct ideas, words, and images. We are passing from Jesus, known "according to the flesh,"[35] to Christ, known "according to the Spirit." A total reordering of the ordinary processes of our psychic makeup is also taking place. Any normal psychological process starts with the external senses, passes to the imagination, the feelings, the mind, and then affects the will. A person's entrance into the Mystery, on the other hand, goes in the opposite direction. It starts with the deepest part of

---

[34] Jn 14:21.23; see also 15:1-12; 17:20-26.
[35] "Even though we once knew Christ from a human point of view, we know him no longer in that way" (2 Cor 5:16).

the psyche, then affects the will, which in its turn sharpens the mind and often touches the imagination and affections, thus stimulating the use of symbols to express the whole experience. It is this total inversion of order, this reverse spin, that causes inner turmoil.

Pure purified faith is like a beam of light that conquers by temporarily darkening our intelligence, which explains our experience of *unknowing knowledge*.[36] This unknowingness is a dark, superconceptual knowledge of the truths of faith, that is, of revealed truths. Such a *learned ignorance*,[37] which is the only adequate path to union with God, permits a type of obscure, general knowledge of the divine presence.

This type of awareness of God's presence can, in turn, give way to an awareness of God's absence, which is how someone is aware of *nothing* and knows God as someone unknown, *quasi ignotus*.[38] Thus God's presence is perceived as a felt absence—that is, as a presence grasped by faith as a quasi absence.

The desert experience is a mystical one, and its object is the Mystery of the glorified Lord. Although it is a concrete mystical experience that most typically happens during the time of prayer, it goes beyond prayer, and thus we can distinguish mystical life from mystical prayer. At the same time, it is important to distinguish between the desert experience and an experience of depression—that is, between the experience of despondent feelings and a clinical depression. In the desert, and in spite of the presence of despondent feelings, which are always possible, there is a sense of being on a journey-toward. In this desert we periodically see the fruits of our conversion and can use our faculties normally when we find ourselves in contexts that are not that of prayer. On the contrary, in a clinical depression one goes around in circles

---

[36] *No saber sabiendo*, "knowing, not to know" (John of the Cross, "Stanzas Concerning an Ecstasy Experienced in High Contemplation").

[37] The phrase *docta ignorantia* is originally from Gregory the Great (*Dialogues*, III, 37, 20), who also describes young Saint Benedict as "learnedly ignorant [*scienter nescius*] and wisely unskilled" (*Dialogues*, II, Prol.).

[38] Thomas Aquinas, *Summa Theologiae*, I, 12, 13, ad 1: "Revelation . . . joins us to him as to an unknown [*quasi ignoto conjungamur*]."

without a clear direction, no fruits are produced, and one's attention, since it is centered on oneself, blocks all other types of activity.

Those who are entering by this way into the Mystery have very little to do, because they are being made anew. Their cooperation with the divine work of grace is reduced to

- persevering in humble submission to the Lord;

- abandoning themselves peacefully and lovingly into his hands;

- cooperating, when possible, with simple acts of faith, hope, and love.

Perhaps the best they can do is to pray confidently with William of Saint-Thierry as follows:

> Forgive me, Lord, forgive my heart's impatience for you; I seek your face, by your own gift I seek your countenance, lest you should turn it from me at the last. I know indeed and I am sure that those who walk in the light of your countenance do not fall but walk in safety, and by your face their every judgment is directed. They are the living people, for their life is lived according to that which they read and see in your face, as in an exemplar. O Lord, I dare not look upon your face against your will, lest I be further confounded. Needy and beggared and blind, I stand in your presence, seen by you though I do not see you. And, standing thus, I offer you my heart full of desire for you, the whole of whatever I am, the whole of whatever I can do, the whole of whatever I know, and the very fact that I so yearn and faint for you. But the way to find you, that I do not find.[39]

Unfortunately, not all of us monks or nuns are like William, and many of us give up the journey that would take us through the desert to the depths and joys of the Risen One who is always desired yet never overtaken.

---

[39] William of Saint-Thierry, *Meditations* 3.3.

Desire (*Desiderium*)

The traditional language of contemplative or mystical desire finds its support in Sacred Scripture. For centuries the Psalms have taught us that

> Like the deer that yearns [*desiderat*]
> for running streams,
> so my soul is yearning [*desiderat*]
> for you, my God.[40]

Even more important is Psalm 62(63), which renowned interpreters have thought to be a song of mystical love. It begins with the words

> O God, you are my God, for you I long;
> for you my soul is thirsting.
> My body pines for you
> like a dry, weary land without water.[41]

This psalm is even the guiding element of the entire letter written by Saint Augustine to the noble lady Proba on the subject of prayer.[42] Psalm 83(84) seems to reply to the preceding psalms of desire when it says,

> How lovely is your dwelling place,
> Lord, God of hosts.
> My soul is longing and yearning,
> is yearning for the courts of the Lord.[43]

Monastic tradition also considered the prophet Daniel to have been "a man of desires," *greatly loved* by God,[44] and to have been given the divine light so that he could become a sign of the state

---

[40] Ps 41(42):2.
[41] Ps 62(63):2.
[42] Augustine of Hippo, *Letter* 30.
[43] Ps 83(84):2-3.
[44] Dan 9:23. Instead of "greatly loved," the Latin Vulgate reads *vir desideriorum*, "a man of desires."

of life of those who give themselves *exclusively to God in penance and continence.*[45]

We find in the Rule of Saint Benedict the pairing of *will* and *desire* (*voluntas/desideria/concupiscentia*). The source of this linked terminology lies in Sacred Scripture, where we often find the pair *will/desire,* taken negatively. Thus the text from Sirach "Do not follow your base desires, but restrain your appetites"[46] is a scriptural text referred to several times in the Rule of Saint Benedict,[47] especially in 7.31: "The second step of humility is that a man loves not his own will nor takes pleasure in the satisfaction of his desires." Similarly, the Pauline text "Live by the Spirit, I say, and do not gratify the desires of the flesh. For what the flesh desires is opposed to the Spirit, and what the Spirit desires is opposed to the flesh; for these are opposed to each other, to prevent you from doing what you want"[48] is behind RB 4.59-60: "*Do not gratify the promptings of the flesh* (Gal 5:16); hate the urgings of self-will."

As we can see in these examples from the Rule, the pair *will/ desire* is largely understood in a negative sense. It is a question of the *promptings of the flesh* and the *urgings of self-will*. In RB 4.46, on the other hand, we are told to "yearn for everlasting life with holy desire." However, it is in the chapter on the observance of Lent that will/desire is transformed into a totally positive reality:

> During these days, therefore, we will add to the usual measure of our service something by way of private prayer and abstinence from food or drink, so that each of us will have something above the assigned measure to offer God of his own will *with the joy of the Holy Spirit* (1 Thess 1:6). In other words, let each one deny himself some food, drink, sleep, needless talking and idle jesting, and look forward to holy Easter with joy and

[45] Bernard, *Sermon to the Abbots* 1: "Daniel is the man of desires given over to abstinence and chastity. By being free for God alone [*soli Deo vacans*], he represents the state of life [*ordo*] of penance and continence."

[46] Sir 18:30.

[47] See RB 7.19, 25.

[48] Gal 5:16-17.

spiritual longing [literally "with the joy of spiritual desire,"
cum spiritalis desiderii gaudio].[49]

It is clear that Benedict is here taking his cue from the letter to
the Galatians, for we see there that the second fruit of the Holy
Spirit is precisely *joy*.[50] The Holy Spirit's action, seconded by the
Lenten observance, permits the will's conversion to take place
and our desires to be placed in their original right order. The *joy*
accompanying and following this conversion is a clear gauge of
its authenticity and of the Spirit's presence. In the last analysis,
it is a question of the "inexpressible delight of love" that accom-
panies those who "run on the path of God's commandments, our
hearts overflowing."[51] Here, as in everything else, Lent represents
the entire life of the monk.

In the West, the theme of spiritual desire is intimately associated with Saint Augustine of Hippo. The Augustinian tradition
entered medieval cloisters by means of the liturgy, *lectio divina*,
Saint Benedict's *Rule*, and the influence of Saint Gregory the
Great. In this tradition, the desire for God has the following chief
characteristics:

- The experience of desire is based on the experience of
  absence.

- The alternation between presence and absence sharpens
  desire.

- The moral quality of desire depends on its object.

- Desire is by its nature affective and lies more in the will than
  in the intelligence.

- The desire for God is innate in the human being and is not
  the fruit of a free choice.

- This desire for the divine only finds its full satisfaction es-
  chatologically, that is, in eternal life.

[49] RB 49.5-7.
[50] Gal 5:22.
[51] RB Prol. 49.

The most important feature of Augustine's approach to desire is its ontological nature. He saw that the desire for God constitutes human nature, that all human beings have an innate capacity for God, an orientation toward God that precedes any choice on their part. It is in this sense that humans have been created in the image of God: "You have made us for yourself, and our hearts are restless till they rest in you."[52] Or, as Bernard of Clairvaux says when he speaks of human existence: "So excellent a creature: . . . [man] is capable of eternal blessedness and of the glory of our great God!"[53] The *Catechism of the Catholic Church* tells us that "the desire for God is written in the human heart, because man is created by God and for God; and God never ceases to draw man to himself. Only in God will he find the truth and happiness he never stops searching for."[54]

This ontological desire is at the root of all our desires. It is the radical need that the part has for the whole, that the creature has for the Creator, and that the image has for its faultless exemplar. This ontological desire is fundamentally an openness to the other, characterized by total receptivity. The mutual, complementary attraction of man and woman for one another is, in the concrete, the most forceful manifestation of such a radical desire. Its opposite is the frightful void of a contingent being separated from the whole to which it belongs.

The paradoxical part of the experience of desiring lies in the fact that we cannot desire God unless he is absent, and, at the same time, we cannot desire him if he is not present. Thus, the alternation of presence and absence keeps the flame of our desire alive. As the abbot of Clairvaux says, "Unless we use the utmost vigilance . . ., we shall neither desire him when he seems absent nor respond to him when present."[55] And again, speaking more

---

[52] Augustine, *Confessions* 1.1.

[53] Bernard, *Sermons on Conversion* 15. See also *Song* 27.10: "What a capacity this soul has, how privileged its merits, that it is found worthy not only to receive the divine presence, but to be able to make sufficient room for it!"

[54] *Catechism of the Catholic Church*, n. 27.

[55] Bernard, *Song* 17.1.

experientially: "As long as I live, the word 'Return,' the word of recall for recalling the Word, will be on my lips. As often as he slips away from me, so often shall I call him back."[56]

The search for God by means of desire found its basic justification, together with an adequately expressive vocabulary, in Bernard's inspired book of the *Song of Songs*. When the soul has nothing belonging to itself, nothing that it can call its own, but rather holds everything in common with God, it is called "bride." It is this bride who says: "Let him kiss me with the kisses of his mouth!"[57] "She is the soul thirsting for God, . . . proved to be a worthy bride by . . . her vehement desire" for the Bridegroom.[58]

All monastic tradition developed the theme of desire, *desiderium*, in close relation to the search for God, heartfelt prayer, *intentio cordis* (intention/tension), and the contemplative life. Saint Gregory the Great is the leading figure in this tradition, and *desire* is a key theme for the Cistercian writers of the twelfth century. Bernard of Clairvaux, in particular, who is a fervent disciple of Saint Augustine, teaches us that desire is an undifferentiated psychic force that sparks us to keep seeking more and more intensely for what we lack. Desire expresses the feeling of absence and is a movement that pushes our being toward the absent good. "Every rational being naturally desires always what satisfies more its mind and will. It is never satisfied with something which lacks the qualities it thinks it should have."[59]

Desire is the source and deepest root of love. When we become explicitly aware of it, so that the will can convert it into the search for God, it becomes the loving desire for God. To conclude, we can say that we *are* desire, because God is Desire in us. It is he who awakens our desire so as to satisfy our hope and make it live, and that is why desire is a grace.

---

[56] Bernard, *Song* 74.7.
[57] Bernard, *Song* 1.1.
[58] Bernard, *Song* 7.2; 32.3.
[59] Bernard, *On Loving God* 7.18. See also his sermons in *Song* 58.2; 31.4; 32.2.

The vocabulary of desire in Christian tradition is extremely rich, above all in the patristic, Benedictine, and Cistercian currents. The noun "desire" (*desiderium*) plays itself out in many variations, such as attraction, longing, love, charity, contemplation, espousal (*affectus, languor, amor, caritas, contemplatio, nuptiae*), while the verb "to desire" (*desiderare*) permutates into particular forms like seeking, wanting, sighing for, thirsting for, moaning for, longing for, coveting, weeping for (*quaerere, cupire, suspirare, sitire, gemere, anhelare, inhiare, plangere*).

As we know, the thirteenth and fourteenth centuries witnessed a remarkable outburst of devotion to the humanity of Christ according to the flesh and according to the spirit. This devotion found a favorable climate in the context of a spousal spirituality of desire. Thus, a current of affective mysticism was born, which became incarnate in the lives and experiences of particular women living to the full the teachings of Bernard of Clairvaux and William of Saint-Thierry on the soul as a bride thirsting with the ardent desires of love. Here is a typical text of Bernard's:

> If then, any of us, like the holy Prophet, finds that it is good to cling close to God, and—that I may make my meaning more clear—if any of us is so filled with desire that he wants to depart and to be with Christ, with a desire that is intense, a thirst ever burning, an application that never flags, he will certainly meet the Word in the guise of a Bridegroom on whatever day he comes. At such an hour he will find himself locked in the arms of Wisdom; he will experience how sweet divine love is as it flows into his heart. His heart's desire will be given to him, even while still a pilgrim on earth, though not in its fullness and only for a time, a short time. For when after vigils and prayers and a great shower of tears he who was sought presents himself, suddenly he is gone again, just when we think we hold him fast. But he will present himself anew to the soul that pursues him with tears, he will allow himself to be taken hold of but not detained, for suddenly a second time he flees from between our hands. . . .
>
> Nevertheless, he will not reveal himself in this way to every person, even momentarily, but only to the one who is proved

to be a worthy bride by intense devotion, vehement desire and the sweetest affection. And the Word who comes to visit will be clothed in beauty, in every aspect a Bridegroom.[60]

Such teaching by Bernard and William, along with the new place in society for women and the new vision of their dignity that arose in the twelfth century, are the key to understanding the Benedictine and Cistercian nun mystics of that time.

Beatrice, born in 1200 and prioress of the Cistercian monastery of Nazareth, is an accomplished master in the art of desire. The experience of desire appears very often in *The Life of Beatrice of Nazareth*, written by her community's anonymous confessor and based on the personal diary of Blessed Beatrice. It seems worthwhile quoting a few paragraphs from chapter 8, titled "The Unbridled Fortitude and Vehemence of Her Spirit":

> On the following day, when the solemnity of the blessed protomartyr Stephen is being celebrated, Beatrice understood from raging impetuous spiritual struggles that a new and unfamiliar madness was rising within her. Its flooding was like that of an ocean wave impatient of all restraint, passing beyond its bounds by its great impetus; it boiled up strong and hard in a sudden disturbance as if it would wholly break the strength of her frail body. Her spirit then received this stronger than usual vigor from the desire for eternal things, by the revelation of which she had been refreshed shortly before, as we said. Its impetus was so mighty and strong that it consumed all her bodily strength like a spider's web; or like a strong untamed beast breaking through the fragile pen holding it, it cast her down and thoroughly subjugated her until her weak body could not stand the impetus and almost wholly collapsed. . . . The disease seemed to simulate a kind of frenzy which she bore out of a most fervent fire of love and sheer desire for heavenly things.
>
> Beatrice understood that the spirit within her was thriving with a purity proportionate to the strong assault of the afore-

---

[60] Bernard, *Song* 32.2–3.

mentioned violence and the vigorous impetus of the desire she suffered. . . .

After that, this spiritual insanity calmed down and changed into a wonderful sweetness of love. . . .

At episodic and irregular times and especially when she thought or spoke—or even heard others speak—of the supreme Good, her ever lively spirit would become excited. Immediately she would tremble in all the members of her weak body, and especially in head and heart. Or this would happen also when her insatiable appetite of love, sighing for eternal things, would be unable to get up to attain what she insatiably desired.[61]

In Beatrice, the strength of desire borders on insanity. One wonders if it is a question simply of *epilepsy* or a real frenzy of love. The symptoms can be confusing, and it is safer to discern the case according to its fruits, which seem clearly to have been fruits of transformation in love. Mystical and fraternal love in Beatrice is not pathological, although some pathology could well have been caused by the reckless love of her first years in the monastery, while later her passionate love will invigorate her and restore her to health. What most probably happened was that the mystical gifts received by Beatrice were conditioned by the alternations of a bipolar mood disorder or, to put it more plainly and technically, a manic-depressive disorder. This would let us appreciate the greatness of Beatrice from a new perspective, in that she knew how to interpret this weakness and integrate it into her spiritual journey, which let her establish a love relationship with God characterized by its depth and stability.

Beatrice's experiences are presented to us in a condensed way in her work *The Seven Manners of Holy Love*, which, as she says, "come down from the highest place and which return again to the summit from which they came."[62] She describes seven experiences of love that can occur during the process of growth in Christian life. The experience of active and passive desire is the

---

[61] Beatrice of Nazareth, *The Life of Beatrice of Nazareth*, trans. R. De Ganck, CF 50, nn. 219–21 (Kalamazoo, MI: Cistercian Publications, 1991) 255–59.
[62] Beatrice, *Life*, 289.

key to the whole exposition. These seven experiences of love should be understood not as successive stages or steps but as concentric circles within which the life of love grows and develops. The treatise, however, is carefully structured and can be summed up as follows:

- The *first manner* of love is the desire to live according to the image and likeness, that is, with nobility, purity, and freedom.

First Diptych: Active Love for God

- The *second manner* of love is the desire to love without measure and to serve gratuitously.

- The *third manner* of love is the painful weakness of this desire and the inability to love without measure and gratuitously.

Second Diptych: Passive Love Coming from God

- The *fourth manner* of love is the undeserved experience of divine love.

- The *fifth manner* is the vehement desire to return love for love.

Third Diptych: In the Abyss of God's Love

- The *sixth manner* of love is personal insertion into the life of God, who is Love.

- The *seventh manner* is the ardent desire to live for all eternity the divine life of this God who is Love.

It is important to make clear that the word *minne*, used by Beatrice, which we translate as "love," is of feminine gender and can have different meanings in medieval Dutch and German. It is etymologically associated with the words *memini*, "to remember," and *mens*, "mind,"and originally referred to thinking of the beloved, who dwells in the lover. In Beatrice, it signifies both divine Love—the divine essence and the Word Incarnate—and human love, as well as the experience of being loved by Love and of loving, within his Love, him who is Love.

Now let us look in more detail at a central text in the *fourth manner* of living in love. Beatrice offers us here a description of the soul's first passive experience under the power of divine love, which is nothing less than a restoration of the lost image:

> Sometimes it happens that love is sweetly awakened in the soul, rising up with joy and flowing in the heart without any human collaboration. And then the heart is so touched with tender love, is drawn towards love with such desire, is embraced so cordially by love, is subjected by love so strongly, and is held in love's embrace so lovingly, that it is wholly conquered by love. In this the heart feels a great closeness to God, a substantial clarity, a wonderful delight, a noble liberty, a ravishing sweetness, a great impulse of a stronger love and an abundant fullness of greater delight.[63]

The subject of this first paragraph is love. Love acts and experiences its own action passively. The verbs in the passive voice underline this aspect of the experience, but the soul is not inactive. Quite the contrary, it experiences a transparent clarity, a wonderful happiness, and a noble freedom.

> Then [the soul] feels that all its senses have been sanctified in love, its will turned into love and so deeply immersed and absorbed in the abyss of love that it [the soul] is made wholly into love.[64]

Now the subject is the soul, which undergoes a radical change. Its faculties have been reduced to the dynamic unity of love. Its will has been transformed by love into a state of being submerged in love's abyss. The fullness of the image and likeness of God in the soul is poignantly expressed by saying that the soul "itself has totally turned into love."

[63] Beatrice, *Life*, 303.
[64] Beatrice, *Life*, 305.

> Love's beauty has consumed [the soul]. Love's strength has
> eaten it up. Love's sweetness has immersed it. Love's greatness
> has absorbed it. Love's exaltedness has raised it up and so
> united it to itself that the soul must wholly belong to Love, nor
> should it love anything else.[65]

For a second time the subject here is love. Love's action is felt in
the sensations of touch and taste, and it is easy to discern a eucharistic background. But, unlike the first time, here Love is de-
vouring the creature, rather than the reverse. In this way there
is total union and a total coinciding of wills.

> When the soul feels itself in the superabundance of delights
> and in this great fullness of heart, its mind is wholly immersed
> in love and its body is withdrawn from itself; the heart melts
> away and all its power is consumed. So conquered is it by love
> that it can scarcely sustain itself, and loses its power over its
> members and senses.[66]

Once again it is the soul that is the subject of this last paragraph.
Love has conquered even the body, since the spirit is submerged
in love and abandons the body in a type of ecstasy.

Beatrice's short treatise concludes by leaving the reader at the
threshold of heaven: "There the soul is united to its bridegroom,
and is wholly made one spirit with him in inseparable faithfulness and eternal love."[67] She concludes by expressing a desire
that reminds us of the concluding words of Saint Benedict in his
Rule: "May God lead us all there. Amen."

Of course, human desire is, of itself, ambiguous. Our ontological desire is, in practice, full of treacherous distortions: narcissism
that induces us to identify ourselves with some sublime reality
because we do not accept being a finite creature; megalomania
and fantasies of omnipotence that compensate for our lack of
self-esteem; illusions of every sort. . . . The Spirit has a formi-

---

[65] Beatrice, *Life*, 305.
[66] Beatrice, *Life*, 305.
[67] Beatrice, *Life*, 331.

dable task ahead, working to reorganize, replace, redirect, purify, and transform our desire, and he does it all by alternating in the soul presences and absences, darknesses and lights, deserts and oases.

Our "Lenten" cooperation with this theological and psychological purification has also to be very sensitive to the social context in which we live, and so we should ask ourselves about the influence of our consumer society on the awakening of our needs and desires. To possess and to consume are the driving forces of life in our consumer society, which is characterized by the polytheistic presence of a multitude of seductive little objects and values.

Consumer-oriented advertising, besides informing us about different products, is motivational. It tells us about a product and, at the same time, surrounds it with other values. Thus, for example, Dawn toothpaste is associated with "clean breath," and this is linked to "kisses," then the kisses are ways to a "loving conquest," which in turn is a guarantee of "success," and this is tied to "social recognition," which is guaranteed to lead to a "life of happiness." Such advertising is quite obviously at the service of consumption, and since consumption is always referred to the satisfaction of our desires, apparently innocent advertising is in fact subliminally teaching us what we should desire and what desires we should fulfill in order to be happy!

To add a final word about "desires" in the plural, so as to distinguish them from "desire" in the singular: desires are the misguided fragments that dart out toward finite objects when some bomb has fragmented unified desire. Our desires' targets are the wishful mirages of our own hunger and thirst. Desires are often simply needs that are momentarily satisfied by obtaining their object. Such is the need for food to alleviate hunger, which is momentarily eased by eating; but the tension or need for food will soon come back again.

We call "expectations" the grasping arms of desires that look to the future in order to manipulate it. Satisfied expectations give rise to a feeling of power, and unsatisfied expectations result in frustration. Desires and expectations are usually short-lived. Our "ideas" about lacks and needs are what awaken both our desires and our expectations and keep them alive. Giving up these ideas lets us live simply and desire with a single desire.

In the light of all we have seen, we can state that the spousal mysticism so typical of Cîteaux is a mysticism of desire. At the same time, it must also be said that without asceticism and discernment of one's desires, no spousal mysticism or heartfelt prayer (*intentio cordis*) is possible, nor can there be a human heart stretched out toward God, nor any union of wills in the Love of the Risen Christ.

Spousal Relationship (*Sponsalia*)

Throughout salvation history the covenant between God and his people followed a process of gradual interiorization. From being almost a juridical agreement originally, this covenant gradually became a spousal love relationship, a betrothal, even a marriage, thanks especially to the Hebrew prophets. The theme of the covenant as a spousal relationship began with the prophet Hosea: "I will take you for my wife in righteousness and in justice, in steadfast love, and in mercy. I will take you for my wife in faithfulness."[68] Isaiah, Jeremiah, and Ezekiel will follow in his footsteps, as will the author of the Song of Songs. As we have already pointed out, the experience of the Risen Jesus in relation to his Church and to each one of us is one of spousal love.

Commentaries on the Song of Songs oscillate between literary realism based on experience and more spiritualized allegory. Judaeo-Christian tradition has never denied the value of either of these interpretations, and, in fact, we can speak of three ways to interpret the Song of Songs:

- historical interpretation, in which the poem symbolically describes the relationship between God and his people, either Israel or the Church

---

[68] Hos 2:19-20.

- spiritual interpretation, according to which the poem symbolically describes the mystical relationship between God and the loving soul

- existential interpretation, which sees the poem as describing the erotic relationship between man and woman, thus revealing the gratuitous nature of both human love and divine Love

This last, existential interpretation does not accept any further reduction that would exclusively emphasize either an erotic or a mystical understanding of the Song. The existential interpretation is "symbolic" in the proper sense of the word (*syn-ballein*: "to put alongside"): it puts human love and divine Love together since, though very distinct, they are nevertheless always inseparable.

It is worth noting that the divine name of Yahweh appears only once in the whole Song, although it appears in a very significant place in the Hebrew text, when the bride tells us at the end of the poem that "love is strong as death, passion fierce as the grave. Its flashes are flashes of fire, a raging flame" (literally "a flame of Yah[weh]."[69] This single mention of the divine name is telling us something very important: namely, that the experience of human love between man and woman is—at the same time and without any confusion or division—an experience of God. The fire of human love unifies, consumes, and transforms because it is also a raging "flame of Yahweh." It is not by chance that it is precisely "she," the bride, who speaks these words, because, in the experience of love, the woman is more unified than the man, so that the two loves, divine and human, mix better and more easily in her heart and in her flesh. At the conclusion of the Song, the bride proclaims her faith in the life-giving, "divine" power of love.

Therefore, the existential interpretation of the Song is a true model for the historical and spiritual interpretations. The mystical

---

[69] Song 8:6.

relation with God is similar to the erotic one, although it goes beyond it and fulfills it. Eros and agape are not opposed since without eros, agape evaporates; and without agape, eros becomes crudely inhuman. But just how is a mystical relationship similar to an erotic one? To answer this question, let us look at four themes from the Song of Songs that have been sources of inspiration for our mystical tradition and so have been incorporated and developed by it.

The entire poem of the Song is based on a dynamic progression of seeking, finding, and disappearing. The mystery of eros is different from the mystery of the "other" precisely in that eros seeks in order to find the other, whereas living for the other means finding the other person in order to continue seeking. This means that the uncertainty of the search is prolonged beyond the transitory certainty of finding the person we have been seeking. The otherness between man and woman—in fact, even their union—is a source, at one and the same time, of deep joy and deep pain. There is an abyss of solitude at the heart of communion; then the solitude is apparently overcome by union with the other person, but only to appear again as differentiation.

This paradoxical dynamic explains how the more active transmission of love by the man seeks to reduce his solitude, but it only leads to more solitude, while the loving reception by the woman silences her solitude as long as it does not turn into passive submission. Becoming a mother is the only temporary victory over solitude, but the Song does not sing about that.

Closely related to what has just been said is the striking interplay of seduction that is so typical of an erotic relationship. I say seductive "interplay" and not "deceit" because the latter would lessen the free choice involved. The seductive interplay ends—to begin again later—with an agreement for union symbolized in the kiss.

A third factor involved is that eros, although presented as blind, has eyes and wants to contemplate. Visual exploration of the other is a school of contemplation and admiration. The images that are used to communicate what is contemplated vary according to the masculine or feminine gender of the object. The woman's eros is fed by her memory, her imagination, and even her dreams, all of which produce a great wealth of symbolic imagery.

Last but not least, the poem and its love relationship reach their climax in the experience of mutual belonging: "My beloved is mine and I am his." [70] These words refer us directly both to Adam and to Yahweh: to Adam when he exclaims, "This at last is bone of my bones and flesh of my flesh," [71] and to Yahweh in the covenant formula between the Lord and his people, when God exclaims, "Obey my voice, and I will be your God, and you shall be my people." [72] This confession of reciprocal belonging and intimate communion is the heart of the mystical interpretation of the Song of Songs as a wedding song between God and each person belonging to him.

It would at first appear excessive to speak of "spousal spirituality" in connection with the Rule of Saint Benedict. And yet there are certain signs that make us wonder how inappropriate the connection might after all be. At the end of the Prologue, the patriarch of monks says: "Never swerving from his instructions, then, but faithfully observing his teaching in the monastery until death, we shall through patience share in the sufferings of Christ that we may deserve also to share [*esse consortes*] in his kingdom." [73] Benedict here follows his source, the Rule of the Master, but at one significant point he departs from it. Where the Master speaks of being "joint heirs" of the kingdom, [74] Benedict talks about being "consorts" in his kingdom. We can suspect that behind this intentional change of words there is also a change of meaning and, thus, of values. "Consort" has two meanings: one is an "associate"; the other, a "spouse, especially of a reigning monarch." Which of these two meanings did Saint Benedict have

---

[70] Song 2:16.

[71] Gen 2:23.

[72] Jer 7:23. See also Dt 26:17-18; Hos 2:25; Rom 9:25.

[73] RB Prol. 50.

[74] Following Saint Paul in Rom 8:17: "[We are] joint heirs with Christ—if, in fact, we suffer with him so that we may also be glorified with him."

in mind when he used this term to refer to the divine inheritance of his monks? Given the context of intimate association with Christ in his sufferings, I would tend to think it was the spousal meaning.

We find another example in the ritual of monastic consecration. When there is a reference to not having anything of one's own, Benedict uses the words "well aware that from that day he will not have even his own body at his disposal."[75] The underlying biblical source here seems to be 1 Cor 7:4, where it is stated that neither of the spouses has authority over his or her own body, since they belong to each other. The letter to the Ephesians also remarks: "No one ever hates his own body, but he nourishes and tenderly cares for it, just as Christ does for the church, because we are members of his body. . . . Each of you, however, should love his wife as himself."[76] We can even think that Benedict considers monastic stability to be like a marriage covenant with the community resulting from the covenant already made by God. Besides, the purpose of the monk's dispossession from material goods is the community of the kingdom—that is, the covenant made in the one Body of Christ as this is described in its ideal form in the Acts of the Apostles.[77]

Finally, in RB 28, the chapter on "Those Who Refuse to Amend after Frequent Reproofs," we read the following words taken from Saint Paul: "*If the unbeliever departs, let him depart.*"[78] The spousal context of this Pauline text, of course, is obvious. The same could be said of Benedict's text, because whoever breaks

---

[75] RB 58.25. See also 33.4: "Monks may not have the free disposal even of their own bodies and wills."

[76] Eph 5:29-30, 33.

[77] See Acts 2:44-45; 4:34-35: "All who believed were together and had all things in common; they would sell their possessions and goods and distribute the proceeds to all, as any had need. . . . There was not a needy person among them, for as many as owned lands or houses sold them and brought the proceeds of what was sold. They laid it at the apostles' feet, and it was distributed to each as any had need."

[78] RB 28.7; italics in original. See 1 Cor 7:15: "If the unbelieving partner separates, let it be so."

the spousal covenant with God and with the community is unfaithful to his commitments.

When we talked about desires, we pointed out that Bernard of Clairvaux and William of Saint-Thierry are two medieval authors who have a fundamental importance when it comes to understanding the doctrine of the human soul as spouse of the Word. We can say that Saint Bernard is the first writer to present mysticism in a coherent synthesis, as a life of spousal love in the heart of the Church, the great Bride and Mother. Mystical union is purely spiritual. The soul, formed anew by the Word, is conformed to him "in love, as Christ also has loved you. Such conformity weds the soul to the Word, for one who is like the Word by nature shows himself like him too in the exercise of his will, loving as she is loved. When she loves perfectly, the soul is wedded to the Word."[79]

The "one flesh"[80] of wedded human love is the best symbol for this spiritual love, which is why Bernard uses the example of natural marriage to illustrate by analogy the unity of spirit that is the height of spiritual marriage. He does this when he asks, "If marriage according to the flesh constitutes two in one body, why should not a spiritual union be even more efficacious in joining two in one spirit? And hence anyone who is joined to the Lord is one spirit with him."[81] Bernard's entire rereading of the Song of Songs is governed by this principle—namely, the transformation of carnal love into spiritual love, the passage from "one flesh" to "one spirit."[82] Thus, divine grace perfects nature without destroying it.

It is for that reason that Saint Bernard, to avoid misunderstandings in his monastic audience, explains so exhaustively in his commentary on the *Song* that the language of spousal love must be understood symbolically[83] and that the spiritual sense of the

---

[79] *Song* 83.2–3.
[80] Gen 2:24; Mk 10:8.
[81] Bernard, *Song* 8.9. See also 7.2.
[82] 1 Cor 6:16-17.
[83] See Bernard, *Song* 1.8 and 11.

text is more important that its literal sense.[84] He makes this explicit when he says: "Let us not dally outside, lest we seem preoccupied with the allurements of lust, but listen with modest ears to the sermon on love that is at hand. And when you consider the lovers themselves, think not of a man and a woman but of the Word and the soul."[85]

On the other hand, Bernard is very aware that when the happy bride enters into the Bridegroom's bedroom, even though it be infrequently and for a short time, it is only after she has made herself "safe from the call and concern of the greedy senses, from the pangs of care, the guilt of sin and the obsessive fancies of the imagination so much more difficult to hold at bay."[86] Therefore, to understand these texts and, even more, to live the experience they are referring to, one has to have overcome "the world's glamour and entanglements."[87] The one able to enter into the language of the *Song*, or to talk about it, is "only the mind disciplined by persevering study, only the man whose efforts have borne fruit under God's inspiration, the man whose years, as it were, make him ripe for marriage."[88]

We have already said above that the great majority of medieval mystics are female theologians. Theirs is a theology incarnated in a feminine experience, in which there is no abstraction from the body. All of them had a special devotion to the sacrament of the Eucharist, which is the sacrament whose purpose it is to make us one with the Body of Christ until our own bodies have risen from the dead. The Eucharist taught them that the real vocation of the human body is to be a reciprocal gift, a channel of communion, a sign of mutual presence. Jesus in his Blessed Sacrament was for them the greatest mystery of transformation, even bodily transformation, into a love that welcomes and that gives itself. Since they knew how to possess their bodies in holiness and honor, they also knew God and the gift that he makes of his Spirit,

---

[84] See Bernard, *Song* 73.1-2; 74.1-2; 75.1-2; 79.1.
[85] Bernard, *Song* 61.2.
[86] Bernard, *Song* 23.16.
[87] Bernard, *Song* 1.3.
[88] Bernard, *Song* 1.12.

which is why they viewed their bodies as sanctuaries of the Spirit who dwelt in them. Indeed, their bodies shared in the experience of marriage with the Lord, sometimes in his condition of weakness, but at other times in his condition of anticipated glory according to the Lord's power to submit all things to himself.

All this helps us to understand spousal mysticism from another angle. The experience of the women mystics of the Middle Ages has its roots in human affection, which is where the union of man and woman is most strongly expressed in bodily sex. Thus, all of them could identify with the experience of the soul described by Saint Bernard:

> When you see a soul leaving everything and clinging to the Word with all her will and desire, living for the Word, ruling her life by the Word, conceiving by the Word what she will bring forth by him, so that she can say, "For me to live is Christ, and to die is gain," you know that the soul is the spouse and bride of the Word.[89]

In the experiences of Hadewijch of Antwerp, a *béguine*—or "religious woman"—living in the first part of the thirteenth century at the same time as Beatrice of Nazareth and closely related to the Cistercian movement, we find some expressions that, if they are judged from Saint Bernard's masculine point of view, would make us say that she was not yet a person "whose years, as it were, make her ripe for marriage."[90] But it is important not to forget that a woman's spiritual experience is much more complete and unifying of body and eros than a man's experience is. For example, in her seventh vision, which took place at dawn on the day of Pentecost, we read the following:

> My heart and my veins and all my limbs trembled and quivered with eager desire and . . . such madness and fear beset my mind because it seemed to me that I did not give pleasure enough to my Beloved and that my Beloved did not fulfill my desire. . . . All my limbs seemed to become disjointed, one

---

[89] Bernard, *Song* 85.12.
[90] Bernard, *Song* 1.12.

after another, while all my blood vessels writhed. Words cannot describe the desire that filled me at that moment, . . . but here is what I can say about it: I desired to have full enjoyment of my Beloved, and to understand and taste him to the full. I desired that his Humanity should to the fullest extent be one in pleasure with my humanity. . . . I wished he might content me interiorly with his Godhead, in one spirit. . . .

He came down from the altar under the appearance of a three-year-old child, turned to me and with his right hand took his Body from the ciborium. With his left hand he took a chalice . . . and simultaneously came with the tunic and gestures of the man he was when he gave us his Body for the first time. He looked like a human being, an attractive, handsome man with a radiant face. . . . He gave himself to me as usual under the signs and species of the Sacrament. . . . Then he came over, took me entirely into his arms and pressed me to himself so that all my bodily members felt the parts of his body, just as he wanted and my heart and humanity desired. So I received in my body the fulfillment of all enjoyment. I was in myself and experienced this for a certain time, but then shortly afterwards, the handsome man outside me disappeared. The contours of his body disappeared from my eyes. I saw him vanish and I sank into the blessed bosom of his love, remaining there swallowed up and lost to such an extent that I could not recognize or perceive him outside me. He was inside me spiritually, inseparably, and I could not have distinguished him from me. At that moment it seemed to me that we were one without any difference between us. . . .

That is how I entered into my Beloved. I wholly melted away in him and nothing any longer remained to me of myself.[91]

We should note here the movement from outside to inside and from existing in oneself to going out of oneself. When she received Communion, Hadewijch experienced Jesus exteriorly in

---

[91] Hadewijch of Antwerp, *Vision 7*, in *Hadewijch: The Complete Works*, trans. Columba Hart (New York: Paulist Press, 1980). The translations of Hadewijch used in this chapter are those of Hart, incorporating the nuances suggested by the author and by John Giles Milhaven in *Hadewijch and Her Sisters: Other Ways of Loving and Knowing* (Albany, New York University Press, 1993) 21.

her body and interiorly in her soul. This twofold union is crowned by undifferentiated union: "one without any difference between us." She cannot be totally in God without being totally taken out of herself, but this total fusion does not annihilate the human subject. There always remains a capacity to perceive an awareness that lets one taste God in the complete union with him. The union is undifferentiated, although the two subjects continue to exist.

The language of Hadewijch's *Letters* seems to be more sober than that of her *Visions,* perhaps because the former have a more pedagogical purpose. Be that as it may, it is still easy to perceive the unity of her whole being in her spiritual experience. Here are two revealing paragraphs:

> May God make known to you, dear child, who he is, and how he deals with his servants, and especially with his hand-maids—and may he submerge you in him.
>
> Where the abyss of his wisdom is, he will teach you what he is, and with what wondrous sweetness one loved dwells in the other, and how they penetrate each other in a way that neither of the two distinguishes himself from the other. But they mutu-ally enjoy each other, mouth in mouth, heart in heart, body in body, and soul in soul, while one sweet *divine Nature* flows through them both (2 Pet 1:4), and they are both one thing through each other, but at the same time remain two different selves—yes, and remain so forever.[92]

> For as it is the custom of friends between themselves to hide little and reveal much, what is most experienced is the close feeling of one another, when they relish, devour, drink, and swallow up each other.[93]

Hadewijch uses a key Flemish word here to refer to the satis-faction and appeasement of desire: *ghebrukken,* which means "to enjoy, relish, receive pleasure." Such relatively imprecise transla-tions do not always do justice to the sexual and erotic connota-tions of the original term. According to our Flemish mystic, total

[92] Hadewijch, *Letter* 9; emphasis in original.
[93] Hadewijch, *Letter* 11.

union is experienced as joy, delight, and pleasure, but this delightful possession (*ghebrukken*) is lived in continual alternation with a painful dispossession (*gheberken*), and this is the way one arrives at a deep, stable union beyond the many varying states of soul.

We come now to some texts of Gertrude, nun of Helfta during the thirteenth century, particularly the fifth exercise of her work *Spiritual Exercises*. First, however, a few introductory words are called for. The spirituality of Saint Gertrude, or "Trutta," as she was called in her community, is feminine through and through, and she does not hesitate to change the gender of real persons, or of those who appear in gospel parables, to fit them to her own life situation. Thus, she speaks of herself as a "prodigal daughter"[94] and an "adopted daughter"[95] and goes so far as to take the place of John as she rests like a "little girl (*puellula*)"[96] on the breast of Jesus at the Last Supper. She often refers to God or to Christ using personifications in the feminine gender, such as Goodness (*bonitas*), Loving-Kindness (*pietas*), Wisdom (*sapientia*), and Truth (*veritas*), thus balancing the analogical concepts that refer to God and going beyond any expression bound to one or the other gender.

The fifth spiritual exercise treats of mystical union with the Beloved. We find here a rich variety of mystical language used to express the inexpressible. Following monastic profession and the consecration of virgins treated in the fourth exercise, the nun is aflame with desire for the kiss of her eternal Bridegroom and for the nuptial embrace in the hidden wedding bed of her heart. She attempts to become one spirit with the Lord. There is a revealing echo in Gertrude's language of the strength of eros—that is, of passionate love—but her highly poetic style keeps the reader from falling into useless semierotic sentimentality. Gertrude's love as expressed in her writings is that of a mature

---

[94] Gertrude of Helfta, *Spiritual Exercises* 4.184.

[95] Gertrude, *Exercises* 5.510.

[96] Gertrude, *Oeuvres Spirituelles*, V, Sources Chrétiennes 255 (Paris: Éditions du Cerf, 1986) 257.

woman who has left any youthful frivolities far behind. When she speaks of herself, she calls herself "bride and wife,"[97] in other words, the spouse of a husband, a married woman.

The fifth exercise has two parts. The first part divides the day into morning, noon, and evening, and the second part into seven periods according to the seven canonical Hours of the Divine Office. The exercise is clearly the "art of love by loving," as Gertrude says. In the last analysis, it is a question of putting oneself "at leisure for love (*vacare amori*)," as she explains in her introductory words: "As often as you want to be at leisure for love, . . . with all affection, all devotion and intention, may you join yourself to God in prayer, as if you saw the spouse Jesus himself present."[98]

Let us look at some of the prayers that Gertrude makes in order to dedicate herself to Love:

> O love, to see you is to be in ecstasy in God. To cling to you is to be joined to God by a nuptial contract. O serenest light of my soul, very brightest morning, ah, break into day in me now and begin so to shine for me that by your light I may see light and that through you my night may be turned into day. By the love of your love, O my dearest morning, let me reckon everything that you are *not* as if it were nothing and void. Ah! Visit me now in the morning at daybreak that all at once I may be entirely transformed into you.[99]

> Ah! Admit me to the secret of your charity. Lo! My heart already burns for the kiss of your love. Open for me the private bedchamber of your beautiful cherishing-love. Lo! My soul thirsts for the embrace of intimate union with you.[100]

> Ah! O love, dulcet in [your] kiss, you are that fountain for which I thirst. Behold, my heart seethes for you; if only, if only you, a full ocean, would absorb me, an ordinary drop, into

[97] Gertrude, *Exercises* 3.286 and 5.77.
[98] Gertrude, *Exercises* 5.1–9.
[99] Gertrude, *Exercises* 5.30–37; emphasis in original.
[100] Gertrude, *Exercises* 5.101–4.

yourself. You are my soul's living and most dulcet entrance, through which there may be an exit for me from myself into you.[101]

Ah! O love, may your cherishing-love consummated in me be my end and consummation. When the evening approaches, show me the agreement of the nuptial contract that my heart now has entered into with you. In the countenance of my dearest God, you [are] the light of the evening star. At the time of my death, deign to appear to me, O my dear and very bright evening, that in you I may have the wished-for evening of this my sojourn, pleasantly falling asleep and resting on your breast ([which is] full of all gentleness).[102]

Three centuries later, to avoid making a mistake on this same subject—as well as to avoid being burned at the stake!—Saint Teresa of Avila makes the following clarification:

You've already often heard that God espouses souls spiritually. Blessed be his mercy that wants so much to be humbled! And even though the comparison may be a coarse one I cannot find another that would better explain what I mean than the sacrament of marriage. This spiritual espousal is different in kind from marriage, for in these matters that we are dealing with there is never anything that is not spiritual. Corporal things are far distant from them, and the spiritual joys the Lord gives, when compared to the delights married people must experience, are a thousand leagues distant. For it is all a matter of love united with love, and the actions of love are most pure and so extremely delicate and gentle that there is no way of explaining them; but the Lord knows how to make them very clearly felt.[103]

We can see here that Teresa clearly distinguishes spiritual experiences from bodily ones, but that does not mean that the former do not resonate bodily and sexually. Her experience of transfixion describes it clearly:

---

[101] Gertrude, *Exercises* 5.180-84; brackets in original.
[102] Gertrude, *Exercises* 5.216-24; brackets in original.
[103] Teresa of Avila, *Interior Castle* 5.4.3.

I saw close to me toward my left side an angel . . . not large
but small; he was very beautiful. . . . I saw in his hands a large
golden dart and at the end of the iron tip there appeared to be
a little fire. It seemed to me this angel plunged the dart several
times into my heart and that it reached deep within me. When
he drew it out, I thought he was carrying off with him the
deepest part of me; and he left me all on fire with great love of
God. The pain was so great that it made me moan, and the
sweetness this greatest pain caused me was so superabundant
that there is no desire capable of taking it away; nor is the soul
content with less than God. The pain is not bodily but spiritual,
although the body doesn't fail to share in some of it, and even
a great deal. The loving exchange that takes place between the
soul and God is so sweet that I beg him in his goodness to give
a taste of this love to anyone who thinks I am lying.[104]

The following poem of Teresa's returns to the same theme under
different images:

I gave myself to Love Divine,
And lo! my lot so changed is
That my Beloved One is mine
And I at last am surely His.

When the sweet Huntsman from above
First wounded me and left me prone,
Into the very arms of Love
My stricken soul forthwith was thrown.

Since then my life's no more my own
And all my lot so changed is
That my Beloved One is mine
And I at last am surely His.

He pierced me with his sharpest dart,
Love's arrow straight went through my soul.
So, one with my Creator God,
Another love I cannot know.

---

[104] Teresa, *Life* 29.13.

My being now to Him must go
And thus my lot so changed is
That my Beloved One is mine
And I at last am surely His.[105]

Many of Teresa's mystical experiences, especially the transfixion, reveal a psychological element that can be explained as follows. On the one hand, one's personal self invests all the vital energy that it has available in an activity totally proper to it. The experience is totally transcendent and involves the person's spiritual relationship with God. On the other hand, this same personal self appropriates and elevates that unique source of life that energizes even the most primitive instinctual dimensions of human existence, and then uses them for its own purposes. This fact explains the presence of sexualized, erotic resonances in such spiritual experiences. It could be explained more simply by saying that in a human being all that is spiritual can resonate in the body, just as all that is in the body can resonate in the human spirit. This observation, of course, can also be applied to the experiences of Beatrice, Hadewijch, and many other mystics, both men and women.

It is true that some years later, after her "spiritual marriage," experiences like the ones just described have very little sensual or bodily resonance for Teresa.[106] In general, she confesses that "in his goodness, God has always freed me from such suffering." Teresa is here referring to the suffering caused to her by what has happened to her brother, Lorenzo de Cepeda, according to her letter to him, in which she writes: "Do not pay attention to the painful torpor you tell me about. Although I have not had that type of suffering—since God in his goodness has always freed me from such suffering—I think that it is due to the fact that the delight of the soul is so great that it produces a reaction in our nature. If you do not pay attention to what bothers you,

---

[105] *Ya toda me entregué y di.*

[106] See her *Cuentas de conciencia* ("Matters of Conscience") 54.14: "The sufferings of the spirit are very different from those of the body."

it will pass away with God's help. Some other persons have dis-
cussed such a condition with me." [107] In another letter a month
later, Teresa tells Lorenzo about "a man who was grievously
afflicted because every time he received Communion he was
overcome by most painful torpor." [108] Saint John of the Cross
discusses these same phenomena in *The Dark Night* when treating
the passive night of the senses. [109]

To clarify this matter, we can say that the mystical symbolism
of marriage does not have a sexual content, but sexual union
does have something in itself that goes beyond it and opens it to
the area of mystery and the sacred, as the bride of the Song of
Songs says. [110] This explains why mystics down through the centuries, especially women, have always been aware of the sexual
and erotic overtones that can accompany their mystical experiences. It is, however, something accidental, an echo made by
what is happening on the level of the spirit, something to be
suffered without fear or anxiety as a sign that a process of purification is taking place. It is something that can happen at the
beginning, then fades away and is integrated into the process of
spiritual growth. A mystical experience always has some reference to the union of body and soul, so that Christian mystics of
all times, especially women, often speak of union with God in
terms of marriage, since mystical grace transforms sex and eros
into charity, yet without destroying them.

In the preceding paragraphs we have referred to the sublima-
tion and integration of eros and sex in the experience of spiritual
marriage with God by persons consecrated to him in virginity
or celibacy. Our opinion is that this experience follows a different
pattern in the life of those united to one another and to Christ
through the sacrament of matrimony. The *divinization* of married
persons takes place when "married love is caught up into divine

[107] Teresa, *Letter* 173, to Lorenzo de Cepeda (Jan. 17, 1577) 10.
[108] Teresa, *Letter* 178 (Feb. 10, 1577) 7.
[109] John of the Cross, *Dark Night* 1.4.2.
[110] See Song 8:6: "Love is strong as death, passion fierce as the grave. Its
flashes are flashes of fire, a raging flame" (literally "a flame of Yah[weh]").

love"[111] and when "such love, merging the human with the divine, leads the spouses to a free and mutual gift of themselves."[112] In the sexual act itself, the "language of the body" reaches a mystical dimension "as a deep experience of the *'sacrum'* that seems to be *infused* in masculinity and femininity itself . . ., whose roots plunge precisely into the 'beginning,'[113] that is, into the mystery of the creation of man, male and female, in the image of God, called 'from the beginning'[114] to be the visible sign of God's creative love."[115] In this context, the good wishes expressed by Bernard of Clairvaux in a letter to the Duke and Duchess of Lorraine are especially telling, when he hopes "that they may so rejoice in their pure and mutual embraces that only the love of Christ is supreme in them."[116]

Christian mystical theology for married life is obviously waiting to be developed and formulated. A deep, persevering dialogue will be necessary, but it will always be important that we men listen to the women. We who are sexually celibates and virgins will learn much from those who are married, and all of us must begin to listen to the mystical wisdom of Judaism, Islam, Hinduism, and Buddhism.

We must also listen to the voice of lay men and women of our secularized world. It is a proven fact that many of those who claim to be atheists or agnostics are, without knowing it, looking for God in the deepest human experiences, and it is precisely the experience of the love between man and woman that brings them closer to a religious experience. Transpersonal psychology tells us that persons who have arrived at a fuller human potential—

---

[111] *Gaudium et Spes*, n. 48.

[112] *Gaudium et Spes*, n. 49.

[113] Cf. Gen 1:1.

[114] Cf. Mt 19:8.

[115] John Paul II, general audience, July 4, 1984. See "Aud. 117b, 3" in *Man and Woman He Created Them* (Boston, Pauline Press, 2006) 614.

[116] Bernard, *Letter* 123, in *The Letters of St Bernard of Clairvaux* (Kalamazoo, MI: Cistercian Publications, 1998). This is *Letter* 119 of the critical Latin text (Roma: Editiones Cistercienses, 1957). Where the Latin original says *amplexibus* (embraces), the published English translation says "love."

that is, persons who are "self-fulfilled" or "cofulfilled"—live the sexual act with a person they truly love as a religious, spiritual, and almost mystical experience. Furthermore, these persons hasten to say that, through being plunged into the divine Other by the ecstasy of love, one loses consciousness of one's partner. Thus, the deeply human experience is potentially religious.

At this point an important distinction must be made. A "spousal" relationship is different from the "conjugal" relationship of marriage, and therefore "spousal love" is something different from "conjugal love." "Spousehood," the spousal relationship, is a way for human beings to live reciprocally, complementarily, whereas "conjugality" is more restricted and refers to the concrete mode of living a spousal relationship within the institution of marriage. In the same way, conjugal love is a form of living and showing spousal love, but it is not the only way to do so. Thus, there is nothing that automatically excludes an experience of spousal love for God even in the case of one who has no experience of conjugal love with another person. This fact leads us to the question of the exact nature of a spousal relationship and of spousal love.

We find many elements of our reply in person-oriented anthropology, which describes the human being as a "being in and for dialogue." Experience teaches us that the deepest need of each human person is for the "other" and, more concretely, for the other who is sexually different. By philosophizing a little, we can say that the human being is ontologically in need of another person who is sexually different. This need orients each person toward that other person. Partial rest is found when one becomes installed in the other. Falling in love is a typical case of mutual installment oriented to a shared-life project. Those in love live in a state of reciprocal indwelling, with a shared project of a happy, fruitful life. This is where the spousal relationship is found, as an attitude and mode of being for the other, as a special way of giving and receiving, of mutual belonging and complementary enrichment, as life rooted in and flowing out of the depths of one's own being created in the image and likeness of the triune God. To put it briefly, the spousal relationship means that the human being has been created by love in order to love, to give himself or herself, and to receive. This leads us to say that the spousal model or paradigm lies, above all, in the relation between the genders, that is, between man and woman.

The spousal relationship takes us back to God's project at the beginning of creation. God created the human being as man or woman in sexualized complementarity and in a loving, reciprocal dialogue. That is how he created them, precisely that way, in his image and likeness, which is as a spouse and with spousal capacity. The spousal experience on the part of any human person, therefore, can show by analogy the experience of loving reciprocity within the Blessed Trinity and the spousal experience between God and his human creature. The richness and depth of this human experience justifies the fact that its vocabulary be used as the normal way to speak about the ineffable communion with God while at the same time respecting its mystery.

We are all invited—by the most intimate part of our spousal being, which is God's image and likeness in us—to the divine wedding feast:

> Every soul—even if burdened with sin, enmeshed in vice, ensnared by the allurements of pleasure, a captive in exile, imprisoned in the body . . .—every soul, I say, standing thus under condemnation and without hope, has the power to turn and find it can not only breathe the fresh air of the hope of pardon and mercy, but also dare to aspire to the nuptials of the Word, not fearing to enter into alliance with God or to bear the sweet yoke of love with the King of angels. Why should it not venture with confidence into the presence of him by whose image it sees itself honored, and in whose likeness it knows itself made glorious? Why should it fear a majesty when its very origin gives it ground for confidence? All it has to do is to take care to preserve its natural purity by innocence of life, or rather to study to beautify and adorn with the brightness of its actions and dispositions the glorious beauty which is its birthright.[117]

[117] Bernard, *Song* 83.1.

So it is easy to see that the spousal relationship, understood correctly, is very different from the romantic image one might have of it. Sentimentally romantic males and females are happy to taste the spousal relationship on the level of emotions, imagination, and aesthetics, but without entering into its ontological reality. They thus distance themselves from faith, from the Mystery, and ultimately from any mystical, spousal relationship with the Risen Jesus.

Modern mystical theology has been able to clarify the meaning of "spiritual marriage." Thus, this phrase has come to have a technical meaning, designating a specific state occurring at a precise moment of one's spiritual journey. But what was gained in precision here was clearly lost in the term's symbolic and evocative potential. In some cases it has been even worse, to the point of establishing criteria to discern such a state, criteria that unfortunately measure more the accidental elements rather than what is essential to spiritual marriage. In this situation, the experience of spiritual marriage is not easy to identify, even in the life of many Christians who have totally embraced God's will with a love that is faithful, persevering, and heroic.

In reality, spiritual marriage is the fulfillment of the grace received in baptism, that of being coparticipants of the divine nature. If few persons arrive at such a mature experience, it is not because the experience is strange or exotic, but because few people give themselves entirely to him who gave himself entirely over to them. Few return love for love, and few are ready not to look out for their own interests but to conform their will to the divine will, to the point of becoming a single spirit with God in the Risen Jesus.

Unity of Spirit (*Unitas Spiritus*)

The majority of medieval mystics used a text from Saint Paul to express the purpose of their search for God, or better, their encounter with him: "Anyone united to the Lord becomes one spirit with him [*qui autem adhaeret Domino unus spiritus est*]."[118]

---

[118] 1 Cor 6:17.

For William of Saint-Thierry, there can be no doubt that this one-ness of spirit is the purpose of monastic life. In fact, this Pauline text is the keystone of all his mystical theology. When Bernard of Clairvaux wants to get to the bottom of what spiritual marriage means, he immediately goes to this text of Saint Paul and even dedicates the greater part of one of his *Sermons on the Song of Songs*[119] to clarifying the meaning of these few words of the apostle.

The first thing needed for interpreting 1 Cor 6:17 is to put the text in its context. The whole passage reads as follows:

> "All things are lawful for me," but not all things are beneficial. "All things are lawful for me," but I will not be dominated by anything. "Food is meant for the stomach and the stomach for food," and God will destroy both one and the other. The body is meant not for fornication but for the Lord, and the Lord for the body. And God raised the Lord and will also raise us by his power. Do you not know that your bodies are members of Christ? Should I therefore take the members of Christ and make them members of a prostitute? Never! Do you not know that whoever is united to a prostitute becomes one body with her? For it is said, "The two shall be one flesh." But anyone united to the Lord becomes one spirit with him. Shun fornication! Every sin that a person commits is outside the body; but the fornicator sins against the body itself. Or do you not know that your body is a temple of the Holy Spirit within you, which you have from God, and that you are not your own? For you were bought with a price; therefore glorify God in your body.[120]

For Paul, we belong to Christ in an absolutely exclusive manner because we are *members of Christ*. This union is so real that it makes union with a prostitute inadmissible, and anyone who does unite himself with a prostitute separates himself from Christ, which is the opposite of what happens in marital union between two Christians.[121]

---

[119] Bernard, *Song* 71.
[120] 1 Cor 6:12-20.
[121] See Eph 5:21-33.

It is striking that Paul first says that our "*bodies* are members of Christ" and then says that "anyone united to the Lord becomes one *spirit* with him." We could perhaps have anticipated that he would say, "one *body* with him." Probably, Paul, having emphasized the physical realism of the Christian's union with Christ, wants to avoid having this realism understood too materialistically. In any case, the words *body* and *spirit* mutually evoke each other. Using them both avoids a physical understanding of the union without diminishing its realism. At the same time, Paul is telling us that the union with a prostitute is a carnal union with nothing spiritual about it. On the other hand, union in a single spirit makes us think of the Holy Spirit and the new life received through union with Christ.

To sum up, *one spirit with the Lord* signifies two realities: a very real union with Christ and a union involving both the human spirit and the divine Spirit. Obviously, Paul is presenting not merely a doctrine but also somehow his own experience. Otherwise why would he use these words precisely in Corinth, which was a city famous for its free and easy lifestyle?

Let us look now at a few witnesses from tradition. Our interest is both in our ordinary, daily experience and in the invitation to a sublime, sporadic experience. We are in fact one spirit with the Lord and spouses of Christ. We are images of God being restored in his likeness, even though we do not always experience what we are. Thus, for writers like Bernard of Clairvaux, William of Saint-Thierry, and Aelred of Rievaulx, unity of spirit takes place throughout the whole of Christian life and not only as the culmination of the spiritual journey.

So, as a beginning, let us remember three basic principles masterfully presented by Aelred in his *Mirror of Charity*. The first one is that loving God does not consist in experiencing visits, moments of compunction, consolations, and presences "which are not at all dependent on our will." Loving God has to be judged instead "according to the abiding quality of the will itself. To join one's will to the will of God, so that the human will consents to whatever the divine will prescribes, and so that there is no other reason why it wills this thing or another except that it realizes God wills it: this surely is to love God. The will itself is nothing other than love."[122]

The second principle is that the union of our will with God's is proved in two very concrete ways: namely, *passively*, by putting up with trials, and *actively*, by doing what he has commanded.

And finally, since the love of God is his own will itself, which is simply his Holy Spirit, by whom charity is infused into our hearts, the third principle is that the outpouring of God's charity in our heart is itself the union of our human will with that divine Love. When this happens, his Love transforms our love, making it like itself. Thus uniting it to himself "by the indissoluble glue of unity, it is made one spirit with him."[123]

Now we can pass on to the abbot of Saint-Thierry. For William, the state of unity of spirit—that is, of "the unity of the Spirit in the . . . one Lord"[124]—is the culmination of the process of likeness with God. It is the goal of Christian and monastic life, as a simple reading of his *Golden Epistle* shows: "The fact that a man relishes . . . things makes him wise and it is because he has become one spirit with God that he is spiritual. And this is the perfection of man in this life."[125] But there is more, as we are going to see.

William's most original contribution on this subject lies in the area of pneumatology. Spiritual union with God takes place in the Holy Spirit, who is the unity between the Father and the Son: "May your unity unite us!"[126] The Holy Spirit is the Giver and the Gift; he communicates his unity—between the Father and the Son—and is that unity. Thus, he unites and distinguishes, so that in spiritual union there is mutuality between bride and Spirit:

> Upon this bed are exchanged that kiss and that embrace by which the Bride begins to know as she herself is known. And as happens in the kisses of lovers, who by a certain sweet,

---

[122] Aelred, *Mirror of Charity* 2.18.53.
[123] Aelred, *Mirror of Charity* 2.18.53.
[124] Eph 4:3-4.
[125] William, *The Golden Epistle* 2.287.
[126] William, *On Contemplating God* 11.

mutual exchange impart their spirit each to the other, so the created spirit pours itself out wholly into the Spirit who created it for this very effusion; and the Creator Spirit infuses himself into it as he wills, and man becomes one spirit with God.[127]

Union in the Spirit is changed into an experience when the Spirit infuses *enlightened love*[128] into our spirit. This experience, however, has many forms because the Spirit "breathes in us when, and as, and in such measure as, he wills, and thus conforms and unites our spirit to himself."[129]

It is not strange, therefore, that the eucharistic experience is related to unity of spirit and spiritual marriage. William of Saint-Thierry says in this regard:

> Those who kiss, sweetly mingle their spirits, and count it plea-sure thus to share each other's sweetness. . . . This is what happens when we do what you told us to do in your remem-brance. You could not have ordained a sweeter or a mightier means to forward the salvation of your sons. This is what hap-pens when we eat and drink the deathless banquet of your body and your blood. . . . When you say to the longing soul: "Open wide your mouth and I will fill it," and she tastes and sees your sweetness in the great Sacrament that surpasses understanding, then she is made that which she eats, bone of your bone and flesh of your own flesh. Thus is fulfilled the prayer that you made to your Father on the threshold of your passion. The Holy Spirit effects in us here by grace that unity which is between the Father and yourself, his Son, from all eternity by nature; so that, as you are one, so likewise we may be made one in you. This, O Lord, is the face with which you meet the face of him who longs for you. This is the kiss of your mouth on the lips of your lover; and this is your love's answer-ing embrace to your yearning bride who says: "My beloved is mine, and I am his."[130]

---

[127] William, *Exposition on the Song of Songs* 95.
[128] William, *Nature and Dignity of Love* 12. *Exposition* 94, and see 153.
[129] William, *On Contemplating God* 11.
[130] William, *Meditations* 8.5.

On the other hand, the unifying experience can be more simple and common, as when "the Spouse . . . offers this same kiss to the faithful soul, his Bride, and imprints it upon her, when, from the remembrance of the benefits common to all men, he gives her own special and personal joy and pours forth within her the grace of his love, drawing her spirit to himself and infusing into her his spirit, that both may be one spirit [*ut invicem unus spiritus sint*]."[131]

This last text makes two important statements. First, unity of spirit is not reduced to a brief and sporadic experience of transcendence, and second, it is not limited to a simple description of the highest perfection obtainable by anyone in this life as he or she prepares to receive its fullness in the next life. Union with God takes place in many other moments of human existence, which can therefore be judged to be *mystical*. Either in the context of *lectio divina* or at other times, it can often happen that, under the influence of the Holy Spirit, the remembrance of God's blessings awakens us to the love of God by making us realize that we are loved by him and thus made one with him in the love of the Spirit. The nature of the experience is always the same—namely, union in the Holy Spirit—although its intensity can be infinitely variable according to one's pilgrimage to the Promised Land. In whatever way it might be experienced, however, all the baptized "have the first fruits of the Spirit," who intercedes for us "with sighs too deep for words."[132]

The abbot of Clairvaux gives us his doctrine on this subject, principally in his *Sermons on the Song of Songs*. Unity of spirit, *unitas spiritus*, is the renewal of the divine image in us through the recovery of his likeness by charity.[133] The result is that we are thrust into the very heart of the soul's mystical marriage with the Word of God. The communion is complete and there is full mutual penetration.[134]

---

[131] William, *Exposition* 30.

[132] Rom 8:23, 26.

[133] See especially Bernard, *Song* 71.5.

[134] See Bernard, *Song* 71.6: "The bond between us will be strong and the union complete, for I shall be in him and he will likewise be in me."

Bernard's starting point could not be more promising: "Every soul . . . can not only breathe the fresh air of the hope of pardon and mercy, but also dare to aspire to the nuptials of the Word."[135] This is because of the nobility of the soul's origin, created in the image and likeness of God. But since this nobility of origin is preserved and made more beautiful by righteousness of life and affections, the bride of Love must "renounce all other affections and devote herself to love alone, for it is in returning love that she has the power to love."[136] And "so the soul returns and is converted to the Word to be reformed by him and conformed to him."[137]

> Such conformity weds the soul to the Word, for one who is like the Word by nature shows himself like him too in the exercise of his will, loving as she is loved. When she loves perfectly, the soul is wedded to the Word. . . . Truly this is a spiritual contract, a holy marriage. It is more than a contract, it is an embrace: an embrace where identity of will makes of two one spirit. . . .
>
> Such love, as I have said, is marriage, for a soul cannot love like this and not be beloved; complete and perfect marriage consists in the exchange of love."[138]

And there is still room here for the explicit personal experience of this love: "Happy the soul who is permitted to be anticipated in blessedness so sweet! Happy the soul who has been allowed to experience the embrace of such bliss! For it is nothing other than love, holy and chaste, full of sweetness and delight, love utterly serene and true, mutual and deep, which joins two beings, not in one flesh, but in one spirit, making them no longer two but one. As Paul says, 'He who is united to God is one spirit with him.'"[139] Bernard himself willingly gives us his own testimony:

[135] Bernard, *Song* 83.1.
[136] Bernard, *Song* 83.6.
[137] Bernard, *Song* 83.2.
[138] Bernard, *Song* 83.3 and 6. See also 71.5–9.
[139] Bernard, *Song* 83.6.

I, though dust and ashes yet relying on the words of Scripture,
am not afraid to say that I am one spirit with God, if ever I shall
have been convinced by sure experience that I cleave to God,
after the manner of those who abide in charity, and therefore
abide in God and God in them, feeding somehow upon God,
and being fed by God. For I think that it was about such a union
that it was said, "He who cleaves to God is one spirit with
him."[140]

Nevertheless, he [the Word] will not reveal himself in this way
to every person, even momentarily, but only to the one who is
proved to be a worthy bride by intense devotion, vehement
desire and sweetest affection. And the Word who comes to visit
will be clothed in beauty, in every aspect a Bridegroom.[141]

It is true that the experience of oneness of spirit, *unitas spiritus*,
reaches its fullness in heaven,[142] but it is also true that it can be
experienced on earth as well, even before reaching the perfection
of a spouse of Christ. The ardent desire for oneness of spirit is
fulfilled through the kiss of God's "living, active word, [which]
is to me a kiss, . . . an unreserved infusion of joys, a revealing
of mysteries, a marvelous and indistinguishable mingling of the
divine light with the enlightened mind, which, joined in truth to
God, is one spirit with him."[143]

It is obvious that obedience to God's will is a straight road
toward *conformatio*, being transformed into the shape of Christ,
in the direction of ecstasy in unity of spirit. This very obedience
is already love, even though not lived as an experience of love
or communion. The important fact is this: "We are transformed
when we are conformed. God forbid that a man presume to be
conformed to God in the glory of his majesty rather than in the
modesty of his will."[144] No wonder, then, that Jesus taught us to

---

[140] Bernard, *Song* 71.6.

[141] Bernard, *Song* 32.3. Read the entire paragraph for Bernard's whole experience.

[142] See Bernard, *On Loving God* 15.39; *Song* 26.5; *Various Sermons* 92.1.

[143] Bernard, *Song* 2.2.

[144] Bernard, *Song* 62.5.

pray according to his own lived experience, "Thy will be done on earth as it is in heaven!"

It can be many years before our conformity of wills becomes explicit and felt, but such an experience is a gift from God, who knows the best "hour" and is only looking out for our well-being. There is an abundance of witnesses to this progressive experience, in which the occasional meeting becomes frequent and almost normal, the active search stops because of the more passive encounter, the many forms of mediation are simplified in the Spirit of the one Risen Mediator, and communion in the same likes and dislikes transforms the believer into a lover.

Daily fidelity to *lectio divina*, to the celebration of the Eucharist and the Liturgy of the Hours, is usually the most common place for this encounter—in the unity of a single Spirit—with the Risen Jesus, Bridegroom of the Church and of each of the baptized.[145] During this whole process let us call upon the divine Spirit, saying with William:

> O God, you who are charity, Holy Spirit, Love of the Father and the Son and substantial Will, dwell within us and set us in order that your will may be done in us. May your will become our will, that being ready to do the will of the Lord our God, we may find his law and his order in the midst of our heart. Enlighten the eyes of our heart, that we may contemplate with them the immutable light of your truth until it regulates the order of our changeableness and our changeable and wavering will. May your Bride—that is to say, our soul—by loving you, understand in your very love what she must do with herself. Nay rather, do you who dwell in her as God, you who are yourself your love in her, bring it to pass in her that she shall love you through yourself, O you who are her Love;

---

[145] See Bernard, *Song* 12.11: "Although none of us will dare arrogate for his own soul the title of bride of the Lord, nevertheless we are members of the Church which rightly boasts of this title and of the reality that it signifies, and hence we may justifiably assume a share in this honor. For what all of us simultaneously possess in a full and perfect manner, that each single one of us undoubtedly possesses by participation."

and may you yourself, in her, love yourself through her. And in her, may you do with her and set all things in order, according to yourself.[146]

This prayer lets us find the right place for mysticism in our cenobitic—or more simply, our Christian—context. For Saint Bernard, love, or charity, is one's *common will*, shared with God and with humankind.[147] When one's will is not common to others, only with great difficulty will it be so with God. Love of one's neighbor nourishes and purifies the antecedent love of God, even though it might be weak, and the purified love of God, in its turn, crowns the love of neighbor.[148]

This love of one's neighbor, or *social love*, plays a decisive role in the growth of the spiritual life toward mystical love. There are various diagrams and terminologies for this, but the basic doctrine remains constant:

- three steps of *truth*: truth in oneself, by judging oneself; truth in one's neighbor, by feeling compassion; truth in God, by contemplating him[149]

- four degrees of *love*: love of oneself for one's own sake and thus open to the social love of neighbor; love of God for one's own sake; love of God for his sake; and love of oneself for God's sake[150]

- three *Sabbaths* (or times of rest): resting in oneself, resting in one's neighbor, and resting in God[151]

In the last analysis, "No one has ever seen God; if we love one another, God lives in us, and his love is perfected in us."[152] Simi-

---

[146] William, *Exposition* 1.131.
[147] See especially Bernard's *Sermons for Easter* 3.3 and *Sermons for Christmas Eve* 3.6.
[148] See Bernard, *Various Sermons* 121 and *Sentences* 1.21.
[149] See Bernard, *Steps of Humility and Pride* 6.29–7.20.
[150] See Bernard, *On Loving God* 8.23-11.33; 15.39-40.
[151] See Aelred, *Mirror of Charity* 3.1-6.
[152] 1 Jn 4:12.

larly, those who are "with all humility and gentleness, with patience, bearing with one another in love, making every effort to maintain the unity of the Spirit in the bond of peace"[153]—these are the ones who are clinging to the Lord so as to form *a single spirit with him*. The fraternal charity that unites us is simultaneously communion with God, so that the closer we are to God, who is Love, so much the greater will be the love uniting us to each other.[154]

We can also speak of friendship in relation to mystical communion, union of spirit, and the spousal relationship. Aelred of Rievaulx's treatise on *Spiritual Friendship* would be a good example in this regard. We simply note here that some of the friendships of Bernard of Clairvaux can be thought of as "mystical or contemplative friendships." There is, for example, his funeral sermon on the occasion of the death of his blood brother, Gerard: "My soul cleaved to his. We were of one mind, and it was this, not blood relationship, that joined us as one. That he was my bloodbrother certainly mattered; but our spiritual affinity [*societas spiritus*], our similar outlooks and harmony of temperaments, drew us more close still."[155] Perhaps that explains why Bernard presents the love of the bride for the Bridegroom, the Word, with the features of the love of friendship.

We can conclude our study of unity of spirit by recalling the familiar second invocation of the Holy Spirit in the Third Eucharistic Prayer:

> Look, we pray, upon the oblation of your Church
> and, recognizing the sacrificial Victim by whose death
> you willed to reconcile us to yourself,
> grant that we, who are nourished
> by the Body and Blood of your Son,
> and filled with his Holy Spirit,
> may become one body, one spirit in Christ.

---

[153] Eph 4:2-3.
[154] See Bernard, *Sermons for the Dedication of a Church* 1.7.
[155] Bernard, *Song* 26.9.

Alternation (*Alternatio*)

What we will now consider directly has been more or less implicit in all that we have said so far. The experience of changing moods, interior shifts, and alternating rhythms is the most obvious element in the concrete daily experience of anyone seeking to follow the Lord. This fact may have a human confirmation in the study of biorhythms, in the changeableness of emotional moods and states, and in a thousand physiological, psychological, or contextual circumstances. For us, however, these things are not so important. From the point of view of our faith, we can talk in this connection about a *paschal* experience of gradually entering and continually renewing the Mystery of the Lord.

To do this, we will listen to the teaching of the abbot of Clairvaux, who calls "vicissitudes" or "alternations" these continual changes in our inner spiritual experiences, the often disconcerting rhythm of presences and absences,[156] prosperity and adversity, correction and consolation.[157] When we read the third of his *Various Sermons* (*De Diversis*), we are able to see several important elements of his teaching on this subject. He says in the first place that consolation is very good and desolation is very instructive. In fact, without the alternation between one and the other it is impossible to advance in the school of virtue, and any purification of one's interior vision or desire for God comes to a halt. Moreover, without this continual discipline of first one experience and then the other, one does not arrive at the filial love of God that does not seek its own interests, nor God's gifts, but rather God himself. All things, however, are gained by those who truly seek God:

> My perfection is not based only on your morning visit or on your evening trial, but on both of them together. . . . When your morning grace smiles on me I jump for joy and shout my gratitude for your visit, and when the sun sets it is time for the evening sacrifice, and like the dove in mourning I will weep

---

[156] As in Bernard, *Song* 17.1–3; 32.2; 74.1–7.
[157] As in Bernard, *Song* 21.4–6 and 10–11.

in anguish. In this way, each moment will be of service to the Lord, since "at night there are tears, but joy comes with dawn."[158] I will grieve bitterly in the evening so as to taste the morning joy. . . . The repentant sinner is just as pleasing to the Lord as the fervent just man, and the ungrateful servant is as distasteful to him as the insolent sinner.[159]

Bernard comes back to the theme of alternations on the occasion of an in-depth treatment of it at the beginning of his *Sermon 17 on the Song of Songs*, this time in relation to the coming and going of the Holy Spirit. "Persons who are spiritual or whom the Holy Spirit purposes to make spiritual, never cease to experience these alternations; he visits them every morning and tests them at any moment." Thus is "the work of salvation ceaselessly performed in our inmost being with all the skill and sweetness of the Holy Spirit's artistry." It is important to be sensitive to these alternations because "unless we use the utmost vigilance in attending to these gift-laden visits of the Holy Spirit, we shall neither desire him when he seems absent nor respond to him when present." The reason for his absence is "to stimulate us to a more eager search for him," and his presence is "to animate us. . . . The man who is indifferent to his absence will be led astray by other influences; the man who is blind to his coming cannot offer thanks for the visit."[160]

Later, in Sermon 74, Bernard returns to the subject of vicissitudes in the visits of the Word, giving an example from his own experience. He confesses having been visited frequently by the Word, but in spite of the frequency of the visits, he has never experienced the Word as he was entering or leaving. Actually, he neither entered nor left, since "in him we live and move and have our being."[161] So it is good to know how to recognize his presence. And for this the abbot of Clairvaux offers us some experiential criteria on how the Word behaves:

[158] Ps 29(30):6.
[159] Bernard, *Various Sermons* 3.3–4.
[160] Bernard, *Song* 17.1–2.
[161] Acts 17:28.

He is life and power, and as soon as he enters in, he awakens my slumbering soul; he stirs and soothes and pierces my heart, for before it was hard as stone, and diseased. So he has begun to pluck out and destroy, to build up and to plant, to water dry places and illuminate dark ones; to open what was closed and to warm what was cold; to make the crooked straight and the rough places smooth, so that my soul may bless the Lord, and all that is within me may praise his holy name. So when the Bridegroom, the Word, came to me, he never made known his coming by any signs, not by sight, not by sound, not by touch. It was not by any movement of his that I recognized his coming; it was not by any of my senses that I perceived he had penetrated to the depths of my being. Only by the movement of my heart, as I have told you, did I perceive his presence; and I knew the power of his might because my faults were put to flight and my human yearnings brought into subjection. I have marveled at the depth of his wisdom when my secret faults have been revealed and made visible; at the very slightest amendment of my way of life I have experienced his goodness and mercy; in the renewal and remaking of the spirit of my mind, that is of my inmost being, I have perceived the excellence of his glorious beauty, and when I contemplate all these things I am filled with awe and wonder at his manifold greatness.[162]

Now let us look at the contrary experience—that is, what happens in the human heart when the Word is absent or his presence unfelt:

But when the Word has left me, all these spiritual powers become weak and faint and begin to grow cold, as though you had removed the fire from under a boiling pot, and this is the sign of his going. Then my soul must needs be sorrowful until he returns, and my heart again kindles within me—the sign of his returning.[163]

[162] Bernard, *Song* 74.6.
[163] Bernard, *Song* 74.7.

Why is it that the Word goes away? Bernard replies:

> When I have had such experience of the Word, is it any wonder
> that I take to myself the words of the Bride, calling him back
> when he has withdrawn? For although my fervor is not as
> strong as hers, yet I am transported by a desire like hers. As
> long as I live the word "return," the word of recall for the recall
> of the Word, will be on my lips.
>
> As often as he slips away from me, so often shall I call him
> back. From the burning desire of my heart I will not cease to
> call him, begging him to return, as if after someone who is
> departing, and I will implore him to give back to me the joy of
> his salvation, and restore himself to me.[164]

Do we not see ourselves, too, described in this passage from
Saint Bernard that reflects so faithfully his own experience? Another mystic who deeply incorporated into her own life what she
had learned from others is Hadewijch of Antwerp. In her passionate poetry she illustrates the alternations Bernard has just
described:

> After the tempest, calm:
> that is what we usually see.
> Anger at night, the next day peace:
> so love becomes strong.
> The one Love strengthens in this crucible
> becomes so brash through pain
> that he cries out the challenge: I am all yours!
> There is nothing else, my Love, that will give me life:
> Come, be totally mine![165]
>
> Here is the testimony that I and many others can give
> who live the marvels of Love
> and receive derision
> for thinking we have what Love keeps for himself.
> Since he played with me like that

[164] Bernard, *Song* 74.7.
[165] Hadewijch, *Stanzaic Poems* 3.

I learned to know his ways
and now act differently,
so he can't trick me
by promises or threats.
I want him as he is,
whether sweet or cruel.[166]

Now ardent, then cold,
Now shy, then forward,
Love has many caprices,
but reminds us all the time
of our immense debt
to his exalted power
attracting us and calling us back to him alone.

Now enchanting, then horrible,
now near, then far:
this is supreme joy
for the one who knows and trusts.
Love embraces and hits all at the same time!
Now humbled, then exalted,
Now hidden, then displayed;
to be consumed with Love one day
you must risk and dare until you reach
the point where you quaff
the pure essence of Love.

Now light as a feather, then heavy as lead,
Now shadowy, then bright,
sweet peace, choking anguish,
giving and receiving:
this is the life of those who are lost
in the ways of Love.[167]

The ongoing experience of alternating between consolation and desolation is itself a gauge of the authenticity of one's life in the Spirit. The paschal rhythm, with its passages from death to an ever-greater life, is a clear sign of the Christian authenticity

---

[166] Hadewijch, *Poems in Couplets* 13.
[167] Hadewijch, *Stanzaic Poems* 5.4.

of our experience of progressive penetration into the Mystery of the Risen Lord. Without these alternations it would be difficult for our love to achieve the gratuitous quality so proper to God's own love. It is the only way we can come to love as he loves, looking out not for our own advantage but rather for that of others.

Chapter 6

Conclusions

After looking at the different aspects of mysticism in general, and then at many particular types of mystical experience, it is time for a few words by way of a conclusion. These will go in three different directions: a synthesis consisting of basic statements about what we have seen; a reference to the importance of the mystical dimension in any process of renewal or reevangelization of monastic life; and a mention of the service monks and nuns are called upon to offer as regards mystery and mysticism, on behalf of humanity in general and of the Church in particular.

Basic Assertions

In the first place, it would be good to specify some of the basic propositions advanced so far, without further development, simply in order to synthesize matters and tie up loose ends. The essence of the preceding chapters can be reduced to the following important principles:

- Religion lies at the basis of any human culture, and because mysticism is the originating experience of all religions, it is the soul of any culture.

- The Western countries of the North Atlantic are living through what is not only an era of change, but a change of era.

- Human history teaches us that every cultural crisis or change of era is characterized by being a special moment of religious awakening.

- Contemporary culture in the North Atlantic countries, which can be called "postmodern," is tired of ideologies, moralism, dogmatism, ritualism, and the like. It thirsts for transcendent mystery.

- The purpose of monastic life is spiritual experience, the mystical experience of the Mystery.

- Monastic authors of the Cistercian school, both monks and nuns, besides being mystics, are mystagogues—that is, teachers who introduce us into the divine Mystery.

- The women mystics and teachers of the Middle Ages offer us an incarnated theology and, specifically, a *woman's* experience of the important role played in this theology by the human body with its affects and imagination.

- "Mystery" refers to the deepest dimension of reality, to the ultimate nucleus that gives meaning to everything else that exists.

- Human beings have been created by Mystery and for Mystery.

- From the outset, the Christian Mystery has consisted in the Most Holy Trinity, the incarnation of the Son of God, who redeems the world through his death and resurrection, and the deification of human beings through grace. This Mystery is summed up and fulfilled in the Risen Christ.

- Mysticism, in so far as it is a human reality, is the culminating point of the encounter between contingent being and Absolute Being, between what is finite and what is transcendent, between whatever is created and the Creator.

- Mystical nostalgia is something inherent in human nature, because we have been created after the image of God and are in tension toward the perfection of our likeness to him.

- Christian mysticism is the fulfillment of the Mystery of the Risen Christ in us: he living in us and we living in him.

- Mystics are those persons who enter into the Mystery and are gradually transformed by it/him.

- Every baptized person is a mystic, even though he or she only has an implicit, latent experience of the Mystery and not an explicit one.

- In a more particular sense, mystics are those who experience the revelation of the Mystery through a loving knowledge of it, thanks to a mysterious divine infusion.

- Mystical experience, in so far as it is a highly variable and felt awareness of presence and communication, lies within the normal development of the life of grace and of growth in the theological virtues.

- Christian mystics have their source and origin in the supreme mystic, Jesus of Nazareth.

- The mystical experience of Jesus consists in a continual process of self-identity as Son and discovery of his mission as Savior.

- Jesus' self-awareness as Son sent by the Father has moments of maximum intensity at his baptism, on Mount Tabor, in Gethsemane, on Calvary, and on the morning of his resurrection.

- The experience of the Risen Jesus in relation to each one of us is a spousal one, as Bridegroom, because that is how he experiences the divine plan of salvation.

- The experience of God and the Mystery of God are identical at their highest level: Jesus Christ who, risen from the dead, is himself the Mystery of God.

- Christian mystical experience is the experience of the Mystery of Christ: living, dying, and rising again in him.

- Our basic monastic experience consists in the experience of love as it grows toward God through different stages. It is always an experience of love in its free consent to the divine will.

• Our most common experiences of the Lord's Mystery are those of sweetness, kindness, compunction, the desert, desire, the spousal relation, unity of spirit, and the alternation of consolation at God's presence and desolation at his absence. That is how we enter into the Mystery and are transformed by it/him so as to create communion and be at the service of others.

It is easy to see that the spousal experience of our relationship with the Risen Christ has occupied an important position in our presentation, preceded by the desert experience and by desire, and crowned by the experience of union in a single spirit. There are different reasons for our presenting that primordial relationship this way.

The primary reason is that it seems to me that the experience of a spousal relationship with Jesus Christ, the Bridegroom, is closely related to the Risen Lord's experience in our regard. It is made new every day through eucharistic Communion, which makes us one body, one spirit in the Lord. The spousal relationship also gives a distinctive character to our identity as Christians, an identity that will, in turn, enrich the dialogue with the other major religions and religious traditions. A fourth reason is that the spousal relationship implies integrating our gendered bodies and their eros with their desire to seek and to relish spiritual experience and mystical transformation. It also includes the special qualities of friendship, especially the sharing of values and projects, equality between partners, reciprocity, and mutual indwelling. Last, but certainly not least, is the fact that the spousal relationship somehow reflects the concrete experience of most nuns, at least in the Benedictine and Cistercian tradition. It is not strange that many monks prefer to speak of "unity of spirit" instead of the "spousal relationship," but they are basically referring to the same experience of love as a communion of wills.

Monastic Reevangelization

Monastic life is a life of seeking and finding God in Jesus Christ. In other words, it is a life oriented toward the experience of the Lord. That is how monks and nuns give glory to God and work with him for the world's salvation. This explains why any process of monastic renewal must return to what is essential—namely, steering all one's existence toward the Mystery and the mystical experience that this involves.

As happens at all times of change and crisis, today we speak extensively about renewal, reform, and the refounding of consecrated life. Each one of these expressions emphasizes a different aspect of the phenomenon of conversion and adjustment that the circumstances are calling for. Personally, I prefer to speak of the "reevangelization" of monastic life, a term that seems to me to embrace renewal, reform, and refounding in the following way:

- Reevangelization means renewing our hearts by rooting them in the new covenant with its new commandment of love of God and love of neighbor as oneself. Such a renewal can only be achieved if we follow Jesus in the radical demands of his Gospel. Our rule of life has to become the Beatitudes and ardent cenobitic love, which is the one and only way that our communities will ever become true centers of living communion, a foretaste of the kingdom of heaven.

- Reevangelization also means reforming the historical form, the institutional structures, that our monastic life has, so as to make this historical form culturally—and counterculturally—meaningful. This institutional conversion is a concomitant quality of the interior renewal implied in reestablishing our life on its original spiritual experience. In practice, this requires discerning how appropriate our buildings and financial structures are, rethinking our work program so as to put it at the service of the spiritual objective of our life, and judging the true significance of our presence in relation to the Church and the world.

- Reevangelization includes refounding our existence on the mystical experience that is the foundation of the monastic phenomenon and also of the personal vocation of each one of us. If our life is not established on the solid rock of a personal encounter with Jesus Christ through an ardent, loving faith, then everything will eventually collapse.

It is easy to see that reevangelization is symmetrical to "creative fidelity," and in certain pressing situations this will need to be lived as "faithful creativity." In any case, the most central foundation is our mystical conformity to the Person of the Risen Jesus, which requires our open availability to the work of his Spirit. All the rest will be given to us as well. God grant that the good wishes of Hadewijch of Antwerp be accomplished in us:

> May new light give you new zeal,
> new works, the fullness of new delights,
> new goads of love and a new hunger so immense
> that the new love you have may eternally devour your new
>   gifts.[1]

Serving the Church

I have just said, "All the rest will be given to us as well." By this I was referring to the spiritual service expected from monks and nuns in relation to the "thirst for God" so clearly evidenced in our contemporary cultural context. All persons seeking God, and particularly the local and universal Church, are the beneficiaries of such a service. A warning, however, should be given: no one gives what one does not have, and if, not having, one tries to do so anyway, one will only communicate his or her own misery. Moreover, those who do give what they have only do so because they have previously received it. Here is what Bernard of Clairvaux tells us in this connection from his own lived experience:

> The man who is wise will see his life as more like a reservoir than a canal. The canal simultaneously pours out what it receives; the reservoir retains the water until it is filled, then

[1] Hadewijch, *Stanzaic Poems* 33.

discharges the overflow without loss to itself. . . . Today there are many in the Church who act like canals; the reservoirs are far too rare. So urgent is the charity of those through whom the streams of heavenly doctrine flow to us, that they want to pour it forth before they have been filled; they are more ready to speak than to listen, impatient to teach what they have not grasped, and full of presumption to govern others while they know not how to govern themselves.[2]

The true "friend of the Bridegroom," once he has received love's inrush, pours it out, burning with a love full of good zeal that "fills, floods, flows in a bubbling stream and—sure of what it is doing—pours itself out in a rushing torrent that carries everything along with it."[3] True mysticism is not a private affair but a public radiation of light and love. That, however, does not necessarily mean jumping over the cloister walls or going out on the streets to preach. The soul married spiritually to the Word is fruitful because of the Word, in the same way and for the same reason that the Church is a mother:

> When the Bridegroom perceives, as he always does, that the bride has taken her rest for some time on his bosom, he does not hesitate to entice her out again to what seems more serviceable. It is not that she is unwilling, or that he himself is doing what he had forbidden. But if the bride is enticed by the Bridegroom this is because she receives from him the desire by which she is enticed, the desire of good works, the desire to bring forth fruit for the Bridegroom, for to her the Bridegroom is life, and death gain.
>
> And that desire is vehement: it urges her not only to arise but to arise quickly, for we read: "Arise, make haste, and come." It is no small consolation to her that she hears "Come" and not "Go," knowing from this that she is being invited rather than sent, and that the Bridegroom will be coming with her. . . . She is not therefore aroused against her will when what

[2] Bernard, *Song* 18.3.
[3] Bernard, *Song* 18.6.

happens is already her will: for it is no other than an instilled eagerness to advance in holiness.[4]

But the primacy of service is authentic only when it is based on the deep, joyful desire to be always with the Lord:

> The soul is affected in one way when she is made fruitful by the Word, in another when she enjoys the Word: in the one she is considering the needs of her neighbor; in the other she is allured by the sweetness of the Word. A mother is happy in her child; a bride is even happier in her bridegroom's embrace. The children are dear, they are a pledge of [the Bridegroom's] love, but his kisses give [the bride] greater pleasure. It is good to save many souls, but there is far more pleasure in going aside to be with the Word.[5]

> God went one step further in Mary, Mother of Jesus. "Her will was in such great harmony with God's that he joined not only her will, but even her flesh, to himself."[6]

> The love of Christ, like "a polished arrow, . . . not only pierced Mary's soul but penetrated through and through, so that even the tiniest space was permeated by love. Thenceforth she would love with her whole heart, her whole soul and her whole strength, and be full of grace. It pierced her through that thus it might come down even to us, and that of that fullness we might all receive. She would become the Mother of that Love whose Father is the God who is Love."[7]

> And thus Mary mediates all grace, with her maternal influence being especially felt "if any soul has advanced to the point . . . that she is a fruitful virgin, a star of the sea, full of grace and having the Holy Spirit coming upon her." In such a soul, the Lord "will deign to be born, not only *in* her, but also *of* her."[8]

---

[4] Bernard, *Song* 58.1–2.
[5] Bernard, *Song* 85.13.
[6] Bernard, *Homilies in Praise of the Virgin Mary* 3.4.
[7] Bernard, *Song* 29.8.
[8] Bernard, *On Christmas Eve* 6.11.

As a final word, it can be said that "anyone who cleaves to God is one spirit with him. He who has this kind of love is ready to die for his brothers."[9] Charity, "communion of wills," is the synthesis of spousal relationship and parenthood, of prayer and action, of contemplation and service, of mysticism and commitment.

Our warning—that no one can give what he or she does not have—has extended beyond what we had originally planned; but now we can finally add a few words about our monastic service to the Church and to the world.

The first thing to be said is that, in the communion of the Church, all charisms and ways of life are related in intimate solidarity to one another. Thus, no one is outside the life or mission of the Church on the basis of the charism or grace that person has received.

It is clear from all we have seen that our first contribution to the Church and the world is on the level of who and what we are—our simple existence centered directly on the Mystery. This unity of orientation requires a simple, unified life, which fundamentally constitutes a dimension of every form of Christian life and—we say it without hesitation—of all authentically human life. The human being is a combination of the finite and the infinite. Human existence is bestowed on each person by another higher Existence and makes that person's mystery to be greater than the person's own self. In this sense, the living witness of monks, nuns, and monasteries challenges every believer and even nonbeliever searching for authenticity. The price paid for this type of witness is that monasticism as such, and monks and nuns in particular, should be what we are called to be.

Monastic history teaches us that the spiritual experience, from which it originally sprang and through which it flourished, started looking very soon for institutional structures adequate for prolonging its vitality and for communicating its message in a meaningful way. These institutional forms are changeable and

---

[9] Bernard, *Sentences* 3.92.

are conditioned by times and places. Their validity can be discerned by using two criteria: namely, their capacity for protecting and promoting the original monastic experience, and their ability to be a meaningful witness to the Church and to society at large. Thanks to their visible quality, the mediation of these institutional structures is also a vehicle of a concrete, visible witness, so it is important that such a witness be consistent with monasticism's deepest identity.

The coherence between the monastic project and its meaningful presence produces a type of radiation that becomes stronger and more far-reaching to the degree that monks and nuns are listening sensitively to the culture and to the deepest needs of the persons with whom they live. In a nutshell: love produces radiation. When this love, coherence, and sensitivity exist, the influence of monastic life will flow through its special channels, such as a contemplative liturgy shared with others, retreats in a welcoming guesthouse, participation in the monastic charism by lay persons, the wise spiritual accompaniment that is always needed, and theological reflections based on spiritual experience.

But what most counts in the long run is a unified way of life centered on the one thing necessary: our Lord Jesus Christ, the eternal Son of the Father, born of the Virgin Mary by the work of the Holy Spirit, who died and rose for our salvation. Whatever witness we can give is but a little seed of the kingdom of God, sown in the virginal though ravaged womb of human history.

Selected Bibliography

Quotations from the Second Vatican Council and other official Church documents are from the English translations available on the Vatican website: http://www.vatican.va/archive.

Primary Sources

AELRED of Rievaulx. *Mirror of Charity*, trans. E. Connor, Cistercian Fathers Series, CF 17 (Kalamazoo, MI: Cistercian Publications, 1990).

———. *A Rule of Life for a Recluse*, trans. M. P. Macpherson, CF 2 (Kalamazoo, MI: Cistercian Publications, 1971).

BALDWIN of Ford. *Le Sacrament de l'Autel*, I–II, trans. E. de Solms, Sources Chrétiennes 93–94 (Paris: Éditions du Cerf, 1963).

BEATRICE of Nazareth. *The Seven Manners of Holy Love*, in *The Life of Beatrice of Nazareth*, trans. R. De Ganck, CF 50 (Kalamazoo, MI: Cistercian Publications, 1991) 289–331.

BERNARD of Clairvaux, Saint. *Homilies in Praise of the Blessed Virgin Mary*, trans. M.-B. Saïd and G. Perigo, in *Magnificat*, CF 18 (Kalamazoo, MI: Cistercian Publications, 1981).

———. *On Conversion: A Sermon to Clerics*, trans. M.-B. Saïd, CF 25 (Kalamazoo, MI: Cistercian Publications, 1981).

———. *On Loving God*, trans. R. Walton, CF 13 (Kalamazoo, MI: Cistercian Publications, 1974).

———. *On the Song of Songs*, I–IV, trans. K. Walsh and I. Edmonds, CF 4, 7, 31, 40 (Kalamazoo, MI: Cistercian Publications, 1971–80).

———. *Sermons for Advent and the Christmas Season*, trans. I. Edmonds, W. M. Beckett, and C. Greenia, CF 51 (Kalamazoo, MI: Cistercian Publications, 2007).

———. *Sermons for the Summer Season*, trans. B. M. Kienzle and J. Jarzembowski, CF 53 (Kalamazoo, MI: Cistercian Publications, 1991).

———. *The Steps of Humility and Pride*, trans. A. Conway, CF 13 (Kalamazoo, MI: Cistercian Publications, 1974).

Quotations from Bernard not contained in the above works are taken from *Saint Bernard's Sermons for the Seasons and Principal Festivals of the Year*, trans. by a Priest of Mount Melleray (Dublin: Browne and Nolan, 1923), or as explained in the footnotes.

DESERT FATHERS. *The Sayings of the Desert Fathers: The Alphabetical Collection*, trans. B. Ward, Cistercian Studies Series (CS) 59 (Kalamazoo, MI: Cistercian Publications, 1975).

GERTRUDE of Helfta, Saint. *The Herald of God's Loving-Kindness*, I–III, trans. A. Barrat, CF 35, 63 (Kalamazoo, MI: Cistercian Publications, 1991–99), formerly known as Saint Gertrude's *Revelations*.

———. *Spiritual Exercises*, trans. G. J. Lewis and J. Lewis, CF 49 (Kalamazoo, MI: Cistercian Publications, 1989).

GREGORY the Great, Saint. *The Life of Saint Benedict*, trans. H. Costello and E. de Bhaldraithe (Petersham, MA: Saint Bede's Publications, 1993).

HADEWIJCH of Antwerp. *Hadewijch: The Complete Works*, trans. Columba Hart (New York: Paulist Press, 1980).

ISAAC of Stella. *Sermons on the Christian Year*, I (Sermons 1–26), trans. H. McCaffery, CF 11 (Kalamazoo, MI: Cistercian Publications, 1979).

JOHN of the Cross, Saint. *The Collected Works of Saint John of the Cross*, trans. K. Kavanaugh and O. Rodríguez (Washington, DC: Carmelite Publications, 1991).

TERESA of Avila, Saint. *The Collected Works of Saint Teresa of Avila*, I–III, trans. K. Kavanaugh and O. Rodríguez (Washington, DC: Carmelite Publications, 1976–2008).

THOMAS AQUINAS, Saint. *Summa Theologiae*, I–III, ed. Blackfriars, Cambridge (London: Eyre & Spottiswoode, 1964–75).

WILLIAM of Saint-Thierry. *Exposition on the Song of Songs*, trans. M. Columba Hart, CF 6 (Kalamazoo, MI: Cistercian Publications, 1970).

———. *The Golden Epistle*, trans. T. Berkeley, CF 12 (Kalamazoo, MI: Cistercian Publications, 1971).

———. *Meditations*, trans. Sr. Penelope, CF 3 (Kalamazoo, MI: Cistercian Publications, 1971).

———. *The Nature and Dignity of Love*, trans. T. Davis, CF 30 (Kalamazoo, MI: Cistercian Publications, 1981).

———. *On Contemplating God*, trans. Sr. Penelope, CF 3 (Kalamazoo, MI: Cistercian Publications, 1971).

Secondary Sources

ADNÈS, P. "Mariage spirituel," in *Dictionnaire de Spiritualité*, t. X (1980) cols. 388–408.

ALONSO, S. M. *Vivir en Cristo: El Misterio de la Existencia Cristiana* (Madrid: BAC, 1998).

ÁLVAREZ GÓMEZ, J. "El momento histórico de la vida consagrada," in *En el aprieto me diste anchura* (Madrid: Publicaciones Claretianas, 1992) 127–35; 333–51.

ANCILLI, E., and PAPAROZZI, M., eds. *La Mistica: Fenomenologia e Riflessione Teologica*, I (Roma: Città Nuova, 1984).

ARNOLD, S. P. *Refundación: Contribución a una Teología de la Vida Religiosa de Cara al Tercer Milenio*, Colección CLAR 70 (Bogotá: CLAR, 1999).

BEINAERT, L. "La signification du symbolisme conjugal dans la vie mystique," in *Mystique et Continence* (Paris: Études Carmélitaines, 1952) 380–89.

BLANPAIN, J. "Langage mystique, expression du désir, dans les *Sermons sur le Cantique des Cantiques* de Bernard de Clairvaux," in *Collectanea Cisterciensia* (1974:1) 45–69; (1974:4) 226–47; (1975:3) 145–66.

BOFF, L. *Frei Betto: Mística y Espiritualidad* (Madrid: Editorial Trotta, 1996).

BORRIELLO, L., CARUANA, E., et al., eds. *Dizionario di Mistica* (Vatican City: Libreria Editrice Vaticana, 1998).

BÖCKMANN, A. "Benedictine Mysticism: Dynamic Spirituality in the Rule of Benedict," in *Tjurunga* 57 (1999) 85–101.

BOUYER, L. *Mysterion: Du Mystère à la Mystique* (Paris: OEIL, 1986).

BRESARD, L. "Bernard et Origène: Le symbolisme nuptial dans leurs oeuvres sur le Cantique," in *Cîteaux* (1985:2) 129–51.

CASEY, M. *Athirst for God: Spiritual Desire in Bernard of Clairvaux's Sermons on the Song of Songs*, CS 77 (Kalamazoo, MI: Cistercian Publications, 1988).

———. "Beatrice of Nazareth: Cistercian Mystic," in *Tjurunga* 50 (1996) 44–70.

———. "Mystical Experiences: the Cistercian Tradition," in *Tjurunga* 52 (1997) 64–87.

CHU-CONG, J. *The Contemplative Experience, Erotic Love and Spiritual Union* (New York: Crossroad, 1999).

DE GANCK, R. *Toward Unification with God: Beatrice of Nazareth in Her Context*, CS 121, 122 (Kalamazoo, MI: Cistercian Publications, 1991).

DELESALLE, J. "On Being 'One Single Spirit with God' in the Works of William of Saint-Thierry," in *Cistercian Studies Quarterly* (1998:1) 19–28.

DUPUY, M. "Union à Dieu," in *Dictionnaire de Spiritualité*, t. XVI (1994) cols. 40–61.

ÉPINEY-BURGARD, G., and ZUM BRUNN, E. *Mujeres Trovadoras de Dios: Una Tradición Silenciada de Europa Medieval* (Barcelona: Paidós, 1998).

FAESEN, R. "Beatriz de Nazareth y su mística de las '*Siete maneras de amor*,'" in *Cistercium* 219 (2000) 459–70.

FASSETA, R. "Le mariage spirituel dans les Sermons de Saint Bernard sur le Cantique," in *Collectanea Cisterciensia* (1986:2) 155–80; (1986:3) 251–65.

GALLEGO, T. "Espiritualidad esponsalicia en la Regla de San Benito," in *Cistercium* 218 (2000) 335–40.

GILSON, E. *The Mystical Theology of Saint Bernard*, trans. A. H. C. Downes (London/New York: Sheed and Ward, 1940; Kalamazoo, MI: Cistercian Publications, 1990 [CS 120]).

GONZÁLEZ-CARVAJAL, L. *Ideas y Creencias del Hombre Actual* (Santander: Sal Terrae, 1991).

———. "La postmodernidad," in *Vida Religiosa, Boletín* (1989:6) 164–70.

———. "Postmodernidad y nueva evangelización," in *La Vida Religiosa y la Nueva Evangelización* (Madrid: Claretianas, 1990) 81–99; 251–57.

GRÜN, A. *Mistica ed Eros* (Piacenza: Editrice Berti, 1999).

HECKE, L. VAN. *Le Désir dans l'Expérience Religieuse: L'Homme Réunifié, Relecture de Saint Bernard* (Paris: Cerf, 1990).

JIMÉNEZ DUQUE, B. *Teología de la Mística* (Madrid: BAC, 1963).

JOHNSTON, W. "*Arise My Love . . .": Mysticism for a New Era* (Maryknoll, NY: Orbis Books, 2000).

———. *The Inner Eye of Love: Mysticism and Religion* (New York: Fordham University Press 1997).

———. *Mystical Theology: The Science of Love* (Maryknoll, NY: Orbis Books, 1995).

———. *The Wounded Stag: Christian Mysticism Today* (New York: Fordham University Press, 1998).

KRAHMER, S. M. "The Bride as Friend in Bernard of Clairvaux's Sermons *Super Cantica*," in *The American Benedictine Review* (1997:1) 69–87.

———. "Interpreting the Letters of Bernard of Clairvaux to Ermengarde, Countess of Brittany: The Twelfth-Century Context and the

134   *The Sun at Midnight*

Language of Friendship," in *Cistercian Studies Quarterly* (1992:3) 217–50.

———. "Friend and Lover as Metaphors of Right Relation in Bernard of Clairvaux," in *Cistercian Studies Quarterly* (1995:1) 15–26.

LEBRETON, J., et al. "Contemplation," in *Dictionnaire de Spiritualité*, t. II (1953) cols. 1643–2193.

LONGPRÉ, E. "Eucharistie et expérience mystique," in *Dictionnaire de Spiritualité*, t. IV (1961) cols. 1586–1621.

LOPEZ-GAY, J., et al. "Mystique," in *Dictionnaire de Spiritualité*, t. X (1980) cols. 1889–84.

MAÎTRE, J. *Mystique et Feminité: Essai de Psychanalyse Sociohistorique* (Paris: Éditions du Cerf, 1997).

MARDONES, J. M. *¿Adónde va la religión? Cristianismo y Religiosidad de Nuestro Tiempo* (Santander: Sal Terrae, 1991).

———. *Capitalismo y Religión* (Santander: Sal Terrae, 1991).

———. *Neoliberalismo y Religión* (Estella: Verbo Divino, 1998).

———. *Postmodernidad y Neoconservadurismo* (Estella: Verbo Divino, 1991).

McGINN, B. *The Flowering of Mysticism: Men and Women in the New Mysticism 1200–1350* (New York: Crossroad, 1998).

———. *The Foundations of Mysticism: Origins to the Fifth Century* (New York: Crossroad, 1991).

———. *The Growth of Mysticism: Gregory the Great through the 12th Century* (New York: Crossroad, 1994).

———. "Mysticism and Sexuality," in *The Way Supplement* 77 (1993) 46–53.

MERTON, T. *The Inner Experience: Notes on Contemplation* (San Francisco: Harper Collins, 2003), originally published as articles in *Cistercian Studies* (1983–84).

———. *An Introduction to Christian Mysticism*, MW 13 (Kalamazoo, MI: Cistercian Publications, 2008).

———. *What is Contemplation?* (Springfield, IL: Templegate, 1981).

MIQUEL, P. *Mystique et Discernement* (Paris: Beauchesne, 1997).

MIRONES DÍEZ, E. *Comentario al Libro de Los Ejercicios de Santa Gertrudis de Helfta: Texto* (Abadía de Viaceli: IPC, 1999).

———. *"Trutta," Libertad sin Ira: Gertrudis de Helfta* (Abadía de Viaceli: IPC, 1999).

MOMMAERS, P. *Hadewijch d'Anvers* (Paris: Éditions du Cerf, 1994).

MORITZ, T. "The Metaphor of Marriage in the Spiritual Writings of William of Saint-Thierry," in *Cistercian Studies* (1976:4) 290–308.

MULHAVEN, J. G. *Hadewijch and Her Sisters: Other Ways of Loving and Knowing* (Albany: New York State University Press, 1993).

OLIVERA, B. "¿Escuela del amor místico?" in *Seguimiento, Comunión, Misterio: Escritos de Renovación Monástica* (Zamora: Ediciones Monte Casino, 2000) 283–96.

———. "Monje, mártir y místico: Christian de Chergé, 1937–1996," in *Martirio y Consagración* (Madrid: Ediciones Claretianas, 1999) 111–33.

———. "Mysticism: Key to the Reevangelization of Canonical Contemplative Life," in *The Search for God*, CS 199 (Kalamazoo, MI: Cistercian Publications, 2002) 333–87.

———. "Para una mística cisterciense renovada," in *Evangelio, Formación, Mística: Escritos de Renovación Monástica*, II (Zamora: Ediciones Monte Casino, 2004) 175–86.

———. *Traje de bodas y Lámparas encendidas. Espiritualidad y Mística Esponsal: ¿Caduca o Vigente?* Biblioteca Cisterciense 29 (Burgos: Monte Carmelo 2008).

DE PASCUAL, F. R., MATEO, C., and BELTRÁN LLAVADOR, F., eds. *Mística Cisterciense: Actas del Ier Congreso Internacional sobre Mística Cisterciense* (Ávila: Conferencia Regional Española, 1999).

QUINZÁ LLEÓ, X. *La Cultura del Deseo y la Seducción de Dios*, Fe y Secularidad 24 (Santander: Sal Terrae, 1993).

RAVASI, G. *El Cantar de los Cantares* (Bogotá: Ediciones Paulinas, 1993).

REYPENS, L. "Dieu (connaissance mystique)," in *Dictionnaire de Spiritualité*, t. III (1957) cols. 883–929

SAINTE-MARIE, Joseph de, OCD. *Mistica: Sperienza e Dottrina* (Roma: Teresianum [Pontificio Istituto di Spiritualità] 1977).

SANZ MONTES, J. *La Simbología Esponsal como Clave Hermenéutica del Carisma de Santa Clara de Asís* (Roma: Pontificium Athenaeum Antonianum, 2000).

SCHIANO MORIELLO, L. "Beatriz de Nazareth (1200–1268): Su persona, su obra," in *Cistercium* 219 (2000) 429–43.

SCHOLL, E. "Going beyond Oneself: *Excessus Mentis* and *Raptus*," in *Cistercian Studies Quarterly* (1996:3) 273–86.

SCHÖKEL, L. A. *El Cantar de los Cantares o la Dignidad del Amor* (Estella: Verbo Divino, 1989).

———. *Símbolos Matrimoniales en la Biblia* (Estella: Verbo Divino, 1997).

SCOTT PECK, M. *Further along the Road Less Travelled* (New York: Simon & Schuster, 1993).

SOLIGNAC, A. "Mystère," in *Dictionnaire de Spiritualité*, t. X (1980) cols. 1861–74.

SOMMERFELDT, J. R. "Bernard of Clairvaux on Love and Marriage," in *Cistercian Studies Quarterly* (1995:2) 141–46.

TAMBURELLO, D. *Ordinary Mysticism* (New York: Paulist Press, 1996).

THOMAS, R. *Mystiques Cisterciens* (Paris: OEIL, 1985).

VALVERDE, C. *Génesis, Estructura y Crisis de la Modernidad* (Madrid: BAC, 1996).

VELASCO, J. M. "Aportación de la vida monástica a la pastoral de la experiencia de Dios" (unpublished conference, 2000).

———. *La Experiencia Cristiana de Dios* (Madrid: Editorial Trotta, 1995).

———. *El Fenómeno Místico: Estudio Comparado* (Madrid: Editorial Trotta, 1999).

———. *El Malestar Religioso de Nuestra Cultura* (Madrid: Paulinas, 1993).

———. *Metamorfosis de lo Sagrado y Futuro del Cristianismo*, Aquí y ahora 37 (Santander: Sal Terrae, 1999).

VERDEYEN, P. *La Théologie Mystique de Guillaume de Saint-Thierry* (Paris: FAC-Éditions, 1990).

VILLER, M., et al. *Dictionnaire de Spiritualité Ascétique et Mystique: Doctrine et Histoire* (Paris: Beauchesne, 1937–94).

VOGÜÉ, A. DE. "La conversion du désir dans le chapitre de saint Benoît sur le carême," in *Collectanea Cisterciensia* (1994:2) 134–38.

ZONA, J. W. "Set Love in Order in Me: Eros-Knowing in Origen and Desiderium-Knowing in Saint Bernard," in *Cistercian Studies Quarterly* (1999:2) 155–82.